# YOURS BY CHOICE

TOURS BY CHOICE

# YOURS BY CHOICE

## A guide for adoptive parents

### NEW EDITION

## JANE ROWE

Routledge & Kegan Paul
London, Boston, Melbourne and Henley

First published in 1959
by Mills & Boon Ltd
Revised edition published in 1969
New edition
published in 1982
by Routledge & Kegan Paul plc
39 Store Street, London WC1E 7DD,
9 Park Street, Boston, Mass. 02108, USA,
464 St Kilda Road, Melbourne,
Victoria 3004 Australia and
Broadway House, Newtown Road,
Henley-on-Thames, Oxon RG9 1EN
Set in 10/11 Times by
Inforum Ltd, Portsmouth
and printed in Great Britain by
Whitstable Litho Ltd
Whitstable, Kent
Reprinted in 1984

Library of Congress Cataloging in Publication Data

Rowe, Jane.

Yours by choice.
Bibliography: p.
Includes index.
1. Adoption.  2. Adoption — Great Britain.  I. Title.
HV875.R68 1982        362.7'34'0941        81-19257

ISBN 0-7100-9035-8 (pbk)              AACR2

# CONTENTS

# FOREWORD

*Yours by Choice* has for many years been the only book which satisfactorily leads prospective adopters along the whole complex route they must travel. Step by step Jane Rowe discusses not only the facts people need to know and consider, but also, as Clare Winnicott pointed out in her introduction to the first edition, the importance of 'how everyone concerned with adoption *feels* about it'. This includes the natural parents, the children, and the adopters, and the skill with which these feelings are recognised and conveyed led Clare Winnicott to describe the book as an 'important and unique contribution' to the literature on adoption.

Twenty-two years later Jane Rowe has done something equally unique: she has succeeded in up-dating the book so that it takes account of the many changes in the adoption scene, but without losing one jot of the freshness and vigour of the style nor of the directness of approach which has made the work so valuable to do so many people. In this revised edition she has accomplished the difficult task of keeping the same basic outline but incorporating a considerable amount of new material. When the book first appeared, the children being adopted were almost always healthy babies. Older children and handicapped children previously had a mere three and a half pages devoted to them. In this edition, the current recognition of the need of children of all ages and abilities for permanent families is reflected in the parallel discussion throughout of the themes of 'adopting a baby', 'adopting an older child' and 'adopting a handicapped child'.

Clare Winnicott wrote of the 'wisdom and humanity which pervade the book' and twenty-two years have only widened and

deepened both. Jane Rowe has been at the heart of develop-
ments in child care policy and practice in that period. For twelve
years she was Director of the Association of British Adoption
and Fostering Agencies and in that role was chiefly responsible
for the momentous report 'Children Who Wait' which revealed
how few children who remain in public care more than six
months have any real hope of returning home, and how high the
need is for substitute families for those children. She also served
on the Houghton Committee whose recommendations led
directly to the Children Act of 1975. None of this has made her in
any way more remote from what adoption means to the individual. *Yours by Choice* is packed with lively, often touching
stories and illustrations and one feels throughout that it is written
by someone who not only knows but cares. An example of this is
the new chapter on 'Trials and traumas in older child placement'.
If the book had not already proved its worth over and over again
as a guide for adopters of babies entering the new world of
parenthood, it would do so now for those who take on the task of
being parents half-way through a child's formative years. Such
adopters will be greatly helped to understand what they are
doing – and how they might do it better.

The author has marked the chapter on 'Families of origin', 'the
chapter you must not skip' and rightly so. Probably the last
chapter on 'Explaining adoption' should have the same note on
it, and the two be read together. All the research studies have
shown the vital importance to adopted people of knowing about
their origins, and of learning what they know from their adoptive
parents. Equally it is well known how hard it often is for adopters
to cope comfortably with this aspect of the relationship. They will
find help in the sensitive comments in these two chapters. In fact,
it is unlikely that much of this book will be skipped by any reader,
although each chapter does stand alone and individual topics can
easily be picked out for special study.

Clare Winnicott concluded that 'not only those considering
adopting a child' would value this book, but professional workers
too. She said 'Jane Rowe sets a high standard for social workers --
one which they will feel challenged to live up to.' That is if
anything even more true today than when it was written. Adoption has become an increasingly complex phenomenon and
social workers are very aware of the challenge to them in trying
to ensure the best possible outcome for all the people involved.
Specialist workers will find this book an invaluable tool, and
social workers in a generic service, trying to grasp the essentials

of this one aspect of their work, will welcome such a readable exploration of the subtle and sensitive issues which make up an adoption. In addressing herself to adoptive parents, Jane Rowe has helped clarify the issues for everybody.

Phillida Sawbridge

# PREFACE

Re-writing this book after a gap of twenty years has been an interesting experience. It made me realise how much has changed – not only in the adoption world but in our attitudes and social behaviour. It has also been a heartwarming experience because of the help and advice which has been given me ungrudgingly by many very busy people.

In particular I would like to thank: Hilary Alton, Hedi Argent and Juliet Horne of Parents for Children; John Hilton, National Association for the Childless; Jeanne Kaniuk, The Thomas Coram Foundation for Children; Mary James and Ann Whiteside, Independent Adoption Society; Daphne Batty, Diana Rawstron and John Fitzgerald, British Agencies for Adoption & Fostering; Hilary Chambers, Sheilagh Crawford and Janet Hammond, Parent to Parent Information on Adoption Services.

Last but most of all, I am grateful to my friend Lois Raynor who not only patiently put up with plans spoiled and outings postponed because of the time-consuming demands of re-writing, but who gave much good advice and also painstakingly corrected my errors of grammar and punctuation. If in spite of all these people's efforts mistakes have crept in, they must be my fault.

# CHAPTER I

# What this book is about

Although we have only had legal adoption in Britain since 1926, many changes have already taken place in the adoption scene. At some periods during this half century it has been easy to adopt a child and at others it has been very difficult. No wonder people are often confused or out of date in their thinking.

For quite a long time adoption was regarded with considerable suspicion and looked upon as a risky if not foolhardy enterprise. But as both personal experience and official research studies showed it to be a generally happy and successful way of having a family, it gradually became better accepted. Doctors, friends and relatives began to recommend adoption as the obvious solution to childlessness. The number of adoptions steadily increased until in 1968 more than 14,000 children were adopted by people unrelated to them. Many others were adopted by their step-parents.

This situation was good for those who wanted to adopt since most of them were able to do so. It was not so good for children who differed in some way from the healthy, white infant that most childless young couples were looking for. Babies who had physical or mental handicaps, black babies and those who had passed their first birthday either waited a long time for parents or, more likely, were labelled 'unadoptable'. Older children whose parents could not care for them were seldom even considered for adoptive placement but went to children's homes or foster parents.

Now the situation has changed completely. There are very few healthy babies for adoption, but many more older and 'special needs' children are finding security and happiness in adoptive families. Any child who needs and can respond to parents is now considered adoptable. This is good news for the waiting children. It is good news for some families because becoming a parent to a 'special needs' child is an exciting and rewarding undertaking, but it also presents would-be adopters with a series of difficult decisions.

Adoption has always involved making deliberate choices and asking oneself important questions, including the basic one: Can I accept and love as my own a child born to someone else? Today, if you want to adopt a child, your thinking must often be stretched. You will need to ask yourself: Can I accept, enjoy and love as my own a child who is already of school age and whose early years I have not shared? Or a child of a different race? Or a boy or girl who will need help to overcome or live with a physical or mental disability? How much risk can I accept? Instead of saying: Where is the right child for us? you may need to ask yourselves: Which of the children who need a family could we be parents to?

The purpose of this book is to help with these decisions. It has been written mainly for people who are thinking of adopting a child, but it may also be of use and interest to those of you who already have an adopted family. Its aim is to help in your thinking and to stimulate discussion of all aspects of the subject, so that you can either go forward to adoption with confidence and carry it through with success or else be comfortable with the decision that this method of having a family is not the one for you.

No one should feel any obligation to adopt. There are far more people wanting babies than there are babies needing new families. There are older and handicapped children waiting for families, but neither pity nor duty is a good basis for building a happy parental relationship. Never take a child just because you feel you ought to do so for the child's sake or because your partner wants it. Adoption must be something you genuinely want for yourself as well.

Adoption is a legal process by which the rights and responsibilities for a child are given up by one set of parents and taken on by another. Legal adoption cannot be cancelled, though it is possible for a child to be re-adopted by another family. Adoption is for life, for better for worse, for richer for poorer. Like success in marriage, success in adoption depends on ability to give and take and to accept realities. It is much more than a legal process, it is the creation of a family. It involves deep human emotions and has potentialities for high happiness or deep tragedy. Adoption is an adventure. Like most other worthwhile things in life, it involves taking risks and demands much from us.

'But', people may say, 'why all this fuss about adoption? Other children can't choose their parents and the parents have to accept what they get.' Of course this is true. But adoption is not the same as having a child biologically, and it is no good anyone pretending that it is. Adopted children bring just as much joy as 'home-grown' children and may be even more interesting and satisfying. Adoptive parents and children love one another just as much, though in a slightly different way. Quite often the bond between them is even stronger than usual because both child and parents know that the child was specially wanted for his own sake.

As adoption is a different and special sort of relationship it is not equally satisfactory for everyone. Not every childless couple will want to adopt – nor would they be wise to do so even if there were enough babies available. Many people who would have made excellent parents to their own children cannot successfully take on another person's child 'for always'. Many people who would have made excellent adopters for a healthy baby could not, and should not, undertake the special task of bringing up a disabled child or coping with the emotional problems of a child whose early years have been marked by change, neglect or rejection.

Before a husband and wife can both have a comfortable con-viction that adoption is the right plan for them, much thinking and discussing needs to be done. Every aspect of adoption and their own feeling about it need consideration. Adopters have opportunities for choice which are not given to natural parents; they also face a few extra problems.

The English language creates its own special problems for those who write about families. One cannot always say he or she nor the boy or girl. It would be tedious. So, for the sake of clarity, children are referred to here as he, not because girls are less important than boys, but just because it is easier that way. For the same reason, social workers are referred to as she even though nowadays many of them are men.

No one is likely to find every part of this book equally useful. Some of the questions and suggestions apply to childless couples, some to those of you who already have children by birth or adoption. Some chapters may be of special interest to those concerned with finding families for children and some to rela-tives and close friends of adoptive families. Some sections are concerned with babies and some with older children. Each reader will need to select those parts which seem appropriate and helpful. It is worth remembering, however, that a question which you feel is disconcerting or uncomfortable and which you are tempted to skip over might be the very one that you need to consider most deeply. Too much is at stake for you to ignore signs of possible difficulties ahead or leave unexplored any available source of help.

If the problems that may arise and the dangers to be avoided seem to be stressed here, it is because the best time to consider the future and increase your understanding is before you take a child for adoption. But, if you have already adopted a child without going into all these possibilities, or if you realise that some of your ideas or expectations were misplaced, there is no need for alarm. It is never too late to increase knowledge and understanding or, when necessary, to develop new attitudes and ways of thinking and doing. All parents, adoptive and otherwise, learn as they go along. They all make mistakes occasionally, but most of them bring up their children with pleasure and success. You will too.

# CHAPTER II

# The children available for adoption

As Margaret Collindale (senior social worker and leader of the Adoption and Fostering Unit) made tea and put out biscuits she glanced round the meeting room. She noticed that several people seemed completely absorbed in the *Be My Parent* books which she had laid out, and a pleasant looking middle-aged couple were busy talking to her young colleague George Finney as he pinned up pictures on a big screen covered with photographs of children and families. A young woman who had evidently come alone was looking a bit lost and uncomfortable but a group who had just arrived were chatting to each other and obviously exchanging information.

Margaret could not help wondering whether any of these people might prove to be the right parents for Peter or Jennifer or Alan – the three children who were in the forefront of her unit's concern. Peter was a 9-month-old baby with serious problems of slow development; Jennifer, a lovely blonde 8-year-old was partially deaf and because of this had speech and learning difficulties, and Alan was a black 12-year-old, bright and sensitive but also moody and easily upset. Alan had spent seven years in a children's home after his last foster home broke down, and Margaret and her staff in the Adoption and Fostering Unit felt that time was running out for him. If they could not find an adoption home for Alan soon, he might give up hope of ever having a family and it might then be too late to place him successfully.

The meeting was being held in the social services office of a small city. Those attending had responded to an advertisement in the local paper seeking homes for Peter, Jennifer and Alan.

Margaret Collindale suspected that one or two of the couples were secretly hoping that her department might also have hidden away some healthy, white babies needing adoption. She and George Finney knew these people would be disappointed by what they had to tell them but felt sure that in the end it would be kinder to be realistic even if this meant dashing their hopes. Every month their department, like all adoption agencies, had dozens of letters from couples eager to have a baby or young child. But as the department had only four or five babies to place each year, very few of these applications could be accepted. Some couples like Jack and Annette Green who were now absorbed in reading about 'special needs' youngsters in the *Be My Parent* book, would be able to stretch their thinking to consider older or handicapped children. For others, this would not be appropriate.

Margaret vividly remembered the afternoon eighteen months ago when the Greens had first come to see her. They had recently been told by the consultant at the fertility clinic that they would never have a child born to them because Jack was sterile. The doctor had recommended adoption so Jack and Annette came to the Adoption Unit with high hopes. It was a terrible shock when Margaret explained that no applications for babies were being accepted and that the list was likely to remain closed for at least two or three years. Jack was upset and angry, Annette reduced to tears of misery. Both of them wanted children very much indeed. Margaret Collindale wisely decided that at that moment they were in no fit state to consider adopting a child with special needs – indeed they had not yet got over the shock of the consultant's verdict and were hardly ready to think about adoption at all. So she merely mentioned briefly that there were other kinds of children who needed parents, gave the Greens the names of one or two books to read and urged them to get in touch with a local group of would-be adopters and adoptive parents. She felt that at this point the group would be able to offer Jack and Annette much more help and support than she could.

Nothing more was heard from the Greens until they saw the advertisement and wrote to say that though it would be sad to miss the early years of a child's life, they felt they could enjoy becoming parents to a school-age child and would like to come and talk about it. Margaret was very pleased and immediately invited them to the meeting. She remembered them as a delightful couple who seemed to have a lot to offer as parents. She had had experience of people reluctantly suggesting taking an older child just because they could not get a baby and without really wanting this or ever considering how different it would be. Margaret did not think the Greens were like that. They had seemed honest, thoughtful people and she looked forward to getting to know them better.

WHERE HAVE ALL THE BABIES GONE?

It was time to begin the meeting and to start the discussion off Margaret set out the present situation in regard to adoption. She explained that following the second world war there was a period in which large numbers of babies were born to single girls who were unable to keep them. Although sex before marriage was already becoming rather usual, society as a whole would not easily accept illegitimate children. Housing for single parents was almost unobtainable at that time and social security payments were low. Many, many unmarried mothers felt that they had little choice but to place their child for adoption.

By the early 1970s the pattern was changing. Social attitudes to illegitimacy became kinder, housing shortages eased a little, and welfare payments improved. Whereas the pressure on single mothers had previously been in favour of placing their babies for adoption, now the pressure was on them to keep the child. 'You wouldn't be so awful as to give your baby away would you?' became the prevailing attitude. And so, with greater hope of being able to provide a decent life for their children and with much less social stigma on themselves, fewer and fewer young mothers now decide on the heartbreaking parting which adoption involves.

The much wider availability of reliable contraceptives and the possibility of abortion mean that these days far fewer unwanted babies are being born to mothers who cannot keep them. Margaret Collindale told the meeting that whereas her department used to place twenty or thirty babies a year they now placed only four or five. Since they did not want them all to be only children, some went to families who had already adopted one and this reduced even further the number of couples who could hope to have a baby placed with them.

The situation is much the same for all young children. Many applicants would be eager to accept any healthy pre-school child but few young children in the care of local authorities or child care societies are available for adoption. Nearly all have parents who hope to have them home one day. Waiting lists for pre-school children are almost as long as those for babies. In fact, Margaret said, the only applications which can be accepted right away are those from black couples. 'For them,' she said 'the waiting list is always open because for the present, at least, we badly need more black families.'

At this point a member of the group commented that he had several friends who had adopted children without much difficulty and it seemed very unfair that he and his wife could not do the same. Sensing the real distress that lay behind this gentleman's rather blustering manner, Margaret tried again to explain the position. She pointed out that his friends had probably adopted some years ago. Though there were many more babies available then, no one could say that transferring thousands of babies from one family to another was a usual or even a desirable social pattern. It was really a temporary phenomenon which lasted only a few decades when sexual behaviour and attitudes were badly out of step. 'It's difficult to put this into words that don't sound terribly hard-hearted,' said Margaret, 'but for centuries childless couples had to live with their disappointment and I'm afraid it will have to be that way again even though accepting one's childlessness can be very, very hard. It is really most unlikely that there will ever again be large numbers of babies to be placed for adoption.' 'Some couples,' she went on 'realise that they have each other, their work friends and interests and find that life can be full and satisfying without children. Some decide to wait it out and hope to adopt a healthy baby eventually. For others, adopting a "special needs" child may bring great satisfaction and happiness. So perhaps you would like to hear about that next.'

ADOPTING AN OLDER CHILD

Until fairly recently, any child old enough to walk and talk was considered 'older' and therefore hard to place. Most social workers just did not think of adoption as a possibility for children in care and very few people applied to adopt a child beyond infancy. There has now been such a big change in everyone's thinking that an 'older' child for adoption is likely to be at least 9 or 10 and may even be a teenager.

Many of the children needing parents are those who lost out on adoption in the days when healthy white babies were plentiful. Some were premature, sickly or at risk of developing some abnormality. By the time they were declared fit for adoption they had passed the appealing baby stage and got left behind in residential nurseries, children's homes or foster homes. Prospective adopters tended to ask for girls, so rather more boys are still waiting for a family.

Black and mixed-race babies were definitely hard to place until the mid-1970s and Margaret Collindale used Alan as an example of what happened to many of them. Alan's mother was a young white girl who became briefly infatuated with a very charming young man from Jamaica, but when she found she was pregnant she broke off the relationship. Her parents were very distressed and could in no way accept the idea of a black grandchild, so after Alan was born she asked a local adoption society to find a family for him. When the society failed to do so, Alan came into the care of the local authority. He had two temporary foster homes and was then placed in a residential nursery. When Alan was about 18 months old a long-term foster home was found for him. For a time all went well. He grew into a most attractive child and though his foster parents did not find his temperament easy, they became extremely fond of him. Alas, when he was 5 and had just started school, his foster mother, who was an older woman with grown-up children, became very ill and never fully recovered. Alan had to go to live in a children's home. The housemother there loved him dearly and he came to love her in return, but she retired when Alan was 9 and plans to place him in another foster home fell through. Subsequently houseparents found this once attractive and lovable child to be moody, unresponsive and always in trouble. At school he did poorly although tests showed that he had good basic intelligence.

Margaret and the other staff in the Adoption and Fostering Unit decided that Alan must be considered an emergency case. He had started on a slippery downward slope of poor adjustment, shallow relationships and bad behaviour. If this slide could not be halted, it would be bound to lead to serious future difficulties. This child desperately needed permanent parents who would stick by him offering security, firm guidance and consistent affection.

As she talked about Alan, Margaret looked at the members of the group and wondered if any of them had the love, the determination and the commitment to put this troubled youngster back on the road to a happy and successful future. Knowing Alan's good points, his quick mind, imagination and enthusiasm, she felt certain that he could bring tremendous satisfaction and interest to new parents. She also knew they would have to be strong to cope with the way that Alan would have to test out a new family so as to make sure he could really trust them. They would also have to be able to help him deal with the questions of race and identity which are apt to arise so strongly for a black child who has been brought up in a white environment.

One of the group asked whether children like Alan are always placed in black families. George Finney answered this question by explaining that though more West Indians and Asians are now becoming foster and adoptive parents, there are still not nearly enough black homes for all the black children waiting for families. 'We try to save the black adopters for children who particularly want to be part of a black family,' he said. 'Some of our black youngsters feel strongly about this. Others have always lived in white foster homes or children's homes and have never had an opportunity to identify with the black community. They may prefer to go to white parents. Since most of them are of mixed racial backgrounds, we feel this may be appropriate provided the new family help them to feel proud of their black heritage and can make sure that they can get to know other black people.'

George went on to talk about some of the other 'children who wait'. Often, he said, these are family groups of two or three brothers and sisters who very much want to stay together. Behind them lie tragic stories of family break-up – death, desertion and disorganisation. Having lost their parents these children naturally cling even closer to each other so social workers try hard to find families able and willing to accept more than one child. With obvious satisfaction, George told about one childless couple who had taken four brothers and a sister ranging in age from 12 years to 18 months. He made the meeting laugh as he described some of the upheavals and upsets in the early days when the family were settling down together. 'They, too, can laugh about it now' he said, 'but of course it didn't feel funny at the time. The problems they faced sometimes seemed overwhelming and we all wondered if they would make it.'

Just occasionally children's personalities may be so different or their individual needs so great that it seems best to separate them. Sometimes they may be brothers and sisters in name only, having always been brought up separately. But, in general, parting brothers and sisters is a last resort and if it does have to happen, the hope is that the new families will enable the children to keep in touch.

Few people these days can afford to adopt several children at once. In the Children Act 1975 parliament agreed in principle that adoption allowances should be possible in situations where lack of funds would prevent an otherwise suitable adoption. This part of the act is only just being brought into force, and for a trial period schemes for paying adoption allowances have to be limited to certain agencies. George explained that for the time being at least, when finances are a problem, the best plan may be to arrange permanent foster home placement with the clear understanding that adoption will follow eventually, even if it means waiting until the children are self-supporting. (Children can be adopted right up to the age of 18). Fostering allowances cover the cost of food and clothing and necessary 'extras' such as scout uniforms, school outings and holidays.

'Fostering with a view to adoption' may be the best available plan for many of the older children in care who need permanent new families. When children first have to leave home and come into public care, it is usually hoped that before very long their parents will recover their health or solve their personal problems and be able to re-unite the family. Often this does happen, but in other cases it may become quite clear that the original hopes will not be realised. At this point some parents agree that adoption would give their child the best chance for a secure future. Others cannot face the harsh reality and cling to the idea of getting the child home even if they seldom or never visit and cannot cope with their own life problems.

Until another part of the Children Act 1975 comes into force and a legal process called 'freeing for adoption' becomes possible, many children who would benefit from adoption have to be placed in the less secure relationship of fostering. After a while it may well be appropriate for the foster parents to apply to a court for an adoption order. Some parents will agree to adoption when they see their child happily settled. Others may still refuse consent, but if certain conditions are fulfilled a court can nevertheless grant an adoption order because the law requires that first consideration should be given to the welfare of the child. An increasing number of people are successfully adopting children by this route but, as Margaret pointed out to the group, it does involve a willingness to take extra risks and tolerate a lot of uncertainty. It is also essential that the agency and the prospective foster parents/adopters fully understand each other's plans, hopes and problems.

At this stage in the meeting there was a pause for a cup of tea and general chat, and Margaret and George handed round some leaflets about adoption and fostering. They explained that after the tea break the focus would be on children with various kinds of handicap. During the next few weeks further meetings would be arranged to discuss the needs and problems of older children moving into new families.

## HANDICAPPED CHILDREN

Margaret and George could not help hoping that among those attending the meeting they might find a couple or a single parent for Peter or Jennifer so they were particularly keen to talk about these two children and their needs.

Bringing up a handicapped child is a labour of love. Although taking on the task by choice and with your eyes open may be a very different matter from having the burden unexpectedly thrust upon you, it does require extra qualities of patience, stamina and generosity. In many cases the emotional problems of handicapped children are harder to cope with than the handicap itself.

This was certainly true of Jennifer. At 8 years old she was becoming very aware of the difference created by her deafness. Because her disability did not show, people tended to expect more than she could achieve. Margaret explained that although Jennifer's hearing aid helped a lot, the sounds she heard were distorted and so the child found it a constant struggle to understand what was being said. Often she could not do so. No wonder she had temper tantrums! Her own speech was poor so she had the additional frustration of being frequently misunderstood and normal children sometimes teased and mimicked her.

Jennifer attended a special boarding school for the deaf and returned to a small children's home each school holiday, but this arrangement was becoming increasingly unsatisfactory as most of the staff and children she knew had left. Jennifer was becoming more and more unhappy and difficult. She badly wanted a mummy and daddy who would not only have her at home for holidays but would write letters, send parcels and come to school events like other children's parents. She needed someone to whom her achievements would be important, someone who would encourage her to make the most of her abilities and become a self-supporting member of the community. The teachers at Jennifer's school were confident that she could make rapid progress if she had the right backing. Without parents who cared, they feared her future would be bleak.

Little Peter's problems were different with the main difficulty being uncertainty about his future. Doctors had diagnosed a rather rare condition which usually, but not always, caused quite severe mental limitation as well as certain physical problems. At 9 months Peter was showing signs of slow development and could not yet sit unaided, although his temporary foster parents found him a most lovable and responsive baby.

As George described Peter to the group he stressed the uncertainties of this child's future development. It was possible, he said, that Peter would catch up and be within the normal range of ability, though he might never be very bright at school. More likely, however, he would be quite seriously mentally handicapped, would need special education and never be really self-supporting. Prospective adopters or long-term foster parents would need to think hard about the realities of caring for a retarded youngster as he grew to be a boy, a teenager and then a person with an adult's body and a child's mind.

There are many mentally handicapped children waiting for new families. Quite a few of them suffer from Down's Syndrome (mongolism). Down's Syndrome children are usually happy and affectionate youngsters who have a good capacity for enjoying things. They vary a lot in the severity of their handicap. Some are very limited indeed but others learn to read a little, write their names, can undertake simple tasks and possibly hold down a repetitive kind of job.

Some Down's Syndrome children have additional physical problems such as heart defects but, whereas in the past many died young from infections, modern medicine means that most of them live on into adult life. Until recently Down's children, along with other mentally handicapped children, were all labelled unadoptable but now parents are coming forward to offer their love and care and to reap the rewards of the loving response that these 'forever children' can offer.

Youngsters even more handicapped than this are being placed. George told the meeting about Patsy, a tiny mite of a child with severe mental and physical defects who at 2 years old looked like a baby of 6 months. When Mrs Clark first met her, Patsy had never left the hospital in which she was born. Mrs Clark was visiting her own little girl who was in hospital for a minor operation. She became interested in Patsy lying silent and unresponsive in the next cot, went home with the child on her mind and, as she herself put it, thought about her all night long. From that day on she became determined to do something for Patsy, whose own parents had been so dreadfully distressed by her handicaps that they could not bring themselves to take her home from the hospital or have anything to do with her.

Mary Clark started visiting the hospital regularly and gradually Patsy began to respond a little to her. Next she got permission to take the child to her home for a few hours at a time. For nearly two years she went for Patsy every day, brought her home for a while and then returned her to the hospital. Mary and her bus-driver husband then waged a long battle to get permission from the authorities and from Patsy's parents to become her long-term foster parents. In the end they succeeded and she joined the family to be loved and cherished by the Clarks and their other three children. She is still very frail and tiny and though she can now walk a little she is incontinent and will never learn to speak. In spite of this, Patsy loves life and has a great capacity for joy. Miraculously, though her body and mind are so handicapped, her personality shines through and everyone loves her.

Not many families could cope with a little girl like Patsy but many of the waiting children do not have nearly such serious problems. Some physical conditions can be kept in check with medicine, diet and care. Sometimes an operation will effect a cure when the child is older. A boy or girl may be mentally rather slow but able to lead a perfectly ordinary life. As George and Margaret were at pains to stress to the group, what seems like a major problem to one family, another will take in their stride. Some people cope relatively easily with situations which others would think impossible. The important thing is to find out what would really be involved and then be honest and open about one's strengths and weaknesses, what one can accept and what one cannot.

### SECOND BEST OR SECOND CHANCE?

Some people come to adopt because they know or hear about a particular child who is without parents. Some apply for a child with special needs because they feel that they have something special to offer. But probably most people who adopt youngsters such as Alan or Jennifer or Peter start out with the perfectly straightforward idea of adding a baby or a young child to the family. Like the Greens, they are shocked to discover that to adopt a healthy young child will almost certainly involve at least a very, very long wait and may indeed prove impossible, especially for any couple already well into their 30s.

If when you approach an adoption agency you are told: 'Sorry, we have no healthy babies available, would you be interested in an older or handicapped child?' you may at first have the disagreeable sensation that you are being offered the second best. This really is not so. You are being offered the opportunity to consider doing something quite different.

Given the situation in which many couples seek to adopt the few babies available while thousands of older or disabled children are in urgent need of parents, every would-be adopter needs to ask, what is it about being a parent that matters most to me? Do I really have to experience the bottle-and-nappy stage or could I enjoy parenting a child whose early years may be lost in an unknown past but whose present and future are here to be lived? Could I join the ever-growing band of parents who have experienced the tremendous satisfaction of having helped a troubled youngster learn to love and trust and develop his character and abilities? Could I raise a physically handicapped child to be strong, love him without pity and not be overwhelmed by his pain? Could I take pleasure in the prolonged childhood of a mentally slow child who may never be fully independent and will need my care and support indefinitely?

It is no good going in for this kind of adoption if it just seems a second best. But it does not matter a bit if taking on an older or handicapped child is a second choice. When we think back to important decisions in our lives, our first choice of job or boyfriend was probably a far cry from our final career or choice of marriage partner. A second or even a third choice may well be the right one and the development of adoption services for 'special needs' children may offer you a second chance for parenthood.

# CHAPTER III

# Why people adopt children

Whereas it used to be taken for granted that every normal couple would want children, public opinion now accepts the individual's right of choice. In some social groups at least there is no longer the same pressure on everyone to conform and produce offspring. Many couples now postpone having a family while they get on with their careers, and others decide to remain permanently child-free. We now recognise that people can be contented and fulfilled without the experience of parenthood. In fact if one looks at history and literature it is clear that some of the most successful and creative individuals have been childless. The child-free have more time and energy for each other, for their neighbours, friends and for their community. The child-free by choice may still be a small minority but their numbers are steadily growing.

Those who want children want them for a great variety of reasons, some of which they find hard to explain. Most couples want a family because they enjoy children, feel that life is not quite complete without them and see children as the visible expression of their love for each other. They have a deep craving to love and care for a child and receive love in return and they believe they can offer the affection and security of a happy home. These are sound, unselfish reasons that should lead to a happy adoption experience. None the less it is particularly important for all prospective adopters to ask themselves why they want a child and what they hope a child will do for them. Until they know what they want and why they want it no couple can realistically consider whether adopting a child will satisfy their desires.

In a number of cases where an adoption has not been successful it is clear that the parents have taken the child with selfish or short-sighted motives. These were among the reasons for adoption given by parents of children who were adopted as babies but subsequently developed serious behaviour problems: 'We wanted to fulfil the dying wish of our own son.' 'To be a companion to our own little boy who is a cripple.' 'We thought we should do our duty and help race relations.' 'Our marriage was unhappy and though I wanted a child my husband would not have one.' No wonder these children were unable to feel secure and wanted for their own sake!

When you are considering your own attitudes, ask yourselves whether you feel you can be happy if you do not succeed in obtaining a child. Let's hope you can. People who feel that they must have a child at all costs are not likely to make good adoptive parents. They will expect the child to do too much for them. No child can solve his parents' problems and it is unfair to expect this. Children can add untold happiness and joy to parents' lives, but the only unhappy situation they can cure is a couple's normal longing for a child.

Unfortunately, there are a few people who do not see this. There are women who believe that a child will keep a straying husband at home, but in practice when these men see their wives occupied with a baby they are likely to go out all the more. There are husbands who vainly hope that adopting a child will make a neurotic wife less nervous and self-centred, but they forget such women may not be prepared for the self-sacrifice needed to be a good mother. Children are always hard work and frequently they are worrying and troublesome.

If you are childless and long for a family it is only natural to feel very unhappy at times, to have a lump in your throat when you see a mother with a baby or a small boy skipping past holding his father's hand. Most people would feel that way. But if you feel frustrated, empty and dissatisfied much of the time, or your marriage is not what you hoped and you seem to have few friends, or your work is unsatisfying and life is no pleasure, think twice and then twice more before you assume that adopting a child will put everything right. Unfortunately, experience has shown that in these circumstances adoption almost always makes a bad situation worse.

Successful adoptions grow from happiness and security and a mature desire for parenthood on the part of both husband and wife. Sometimes deep humanitarian concern leads to the adoption of unwanted, disturbed or handicapped children who so greatly need the security of loving parents. If you find that, on balance, you are more concerned with what you can do for a child than with what the child can do for you, then you can feel pretty sure you are starting out with the right approach and can confidently hope for a happy outcome. But you should not allow a generous 'do-gooding' attitude to get out of hand. Adoption lasts a lifetime and humanitarian impulses frequently wear thin unless reinforced with personal satisfaction. Even though the wish to give rather than get should be uppermost in every parent's mind, it is normal and necessary to wish to get something good for oneself out of adopting a child.

## A COMPANION FOR AN ONLY CHILD

Perhaps you already have one child whom you enjoy and love deeply but you are physically unable to have a second. Very likely you had always planned to have several children and now you feel that your one little chick will miss a great deal if he is an 'only' and may even grow up selfish and spoilt. You wonder whether to add to your family by adoption. Or maybe you adopted your first child some years ago and when you applied for a second the situation had changed and no babies were available. Perhaps your adopted child is still asking for a brother or sister and you still feel that the family is too small. Now you have heard that there are older children needing homes and are wondering about this rather different sort of adoption. Mixing 'born' and adopted children and adding older children to an existing family both present certain problems but these can be overcome if they are recognised. Occasionally, however, people try adoption as a cure for a lonely or spoilt child, hoping that a brother or sister will make him more contented and easier to manage. This is nearly always doomed to failure.

The crucial question is do you want the adopted child merely as a companion or do you want him first and foremost for his own sake? Maybe the two children will get along together splendidly with only the normal amount of squabbles and jealousies, share many friends and be very close to one another all their lives. But, like many brothers and sisters, they may be quite dissimilar in outlook and character and each may prefer his own friends and activities. If you adopt a companion who is not companionable, your own child will be disappointed and the poor newcomer will find that he cannot measure up to what is expected of him. This is a very shattering experience for a child.

Even when you truly want the adopted child for his own sake, there is a delicate balance to be struck between making the newcomer feel loved and wanted and not allowing your own child to feel left out and miserably jealous. Felicity and Frank Fox adopted 7-year-old Bobby when their own son, Michael, was 9. Michael had always been a happy, normal boy and his parents never expected him to have trouble in accepting the new brother he had asked for so often. They were very worried, however, in case Bobby did not like them and they put all their efforts into making him feel at home. Both of them gave Bobby plenty of hugs and kisses, they consulted his wishes, gave him first choice of everything. If both children had been in mischief, it was always Michael who was held responsible. Michael very soon began to feel left out and as if his place in the family were lost. He tried to get more attention by acting babyishly and being faddy about his food. When this brought nothing but scolding he started to get noisy, boisterous and demanding, refused to share his toys with Bobby and finally resorted to sly pinches and punches to work off his very natural feelings of jealousy. Fortunately, Felicity and Frank were loving and perceptive parents and when they realised what was happening they were able to sort things out and make each child feel secure in their affection.

Such problems occur rather less often when the adopted child joins the family as a baby than when he comes as an older child. When the new member of the family is beyond infancy, he will already have interests, habits and behaviour patterns that may be very different from those you have tried to teach your other children and, as we shall see later, there are many reasons why children who need new families are usually behind in both emotional development and school achievement. Problems are apt to be at their greatest when the new child is of the same sex and close in age to the child who is already in the family. In fact, it is seldom wise to adopt a child very close in age to an existing member of the family for it is almost bound to lead to rivalry and comparisons. Emotional age is just as important as the number of birthdays. If they are of different sexes and at different stages of development it is easier to help each child to feel successful and the competition is less acute.

It used to be thought most unwise to bring into the family a child older than those already there. There were some sound reasons for this belief. Certainly many of the deprived and troubled youngsters awaiting foster and adoptive families do need to be very definitely the youngest in the family so they do not have to compete and can enjoy being the baby. Recently, however, some families have tried slotting a child into a family gap or taking in one who is considerably older than any of their existing children. This can work out very well if it is done with care.

Laura was 12 when she joined the Russell family and Daniel Russell was only 7. The age gap proved to be just right. Because of the changes and upsets in her early life, Laura was still very young for her age. Under cover of 'minding' Danny, she could behave like a much younger child and Danny did not notice her immaturity or laugh at her because she wanted to play with dolls.

While many eldest children would bitterly resent giving up this position, others find it rather a relief. Being big brother may boost the newcomer's morale and he may show affection to a younger brother or sister more easily than to adults. Each family's situation is unique. What is certain is that everyone's needs and feelings must be listened to and their views taken seriously. Although the final decision about adding a child to the family is one for the adults to make, it would be most unwise to adopt another child, especially one beyond infancy, if your present child does not want this. Adoption is always a family affair.

There are disadvantages in being an only child but it has its compensations too. If your family is a close, happy trio, you will need to think hard before disturbing this congenial state of affairs. Only children can be spoilt and tiresome but there is no reason why yours should be that way if you can prevent yourselves from over-protecting him, fussing about his every movement and making him the centre of the household. If you are the relaxed, warm and understanding parents who will make a good job of bringing up a family you can make a good job of bringing up an only child too.

REPLACING A LOST CHILD

Quite a number of couples in the adoption queue have had a child who died. In their grief they feel that only another child can ease their sorrow. Sometimes they think they want a little girl who can step right into their lost daughter's shoes, take on the piano lessons she had started or excel in the same way in the local ballet troupe. Or perhaps it is the studious, helpful boy who was his mother's pride and joy that they hope to replace. What will these parents feel if their new child shows none of these same interests and characteristics, if the girl is more interested in roller skating than piano lessons and the boy is out with his friends all day getting into mischief? What will the child feel if he realises he is being asked to mould himself to another child's pattern, if he finds he is not wanted for himself but merely because he keeps alive the memory of a better-loved predecessor?

If you have had the tragic experience of losing a child it would be well to wait a few months and to ask yourselves whether you want a completely new personality as a member of your family or a replica of the child you lost. You will not want to find yourselves constantly making unfavourable comparisons between the troublesome flesh-and-blood child in your home and the rather idealised recollection of your first child. If you have other children, they may have strong feelings about a new brother or sister. It is as well to remember also that some families have found it quite unbearable to see another child use the lost child's room or toys.

For some bereaved families adoption would be a serious mistake, but others who have allowed themselves to mourn, analysed their feelings and know that they can enjoy a wide range of children can go ahead with considerable confidence. They know they like being parents and they have both love and experience to offer.

THE POPULATION PROBLEM AND LARGE FAMILIES

Lots of people feel very strongly that we should not be adding to the population pressure on our overcrowded planet yet they would love a big family. The obvious solution seems to be to adopt unwanted children who are already born. This sounds fine but there can be complications.

Martin and Cecilia McC both came from large families. They decided they wanted at least four children and would have two and then adopt two. They also wanted them to be close in age – partly for the children's sake and partly because Cecilia hoped to pick up her career again once all the children were in school. So when their little boys were 3 and 5 they applied to a big child care society to adopt a child of either sex and any colour but not more than 5 years old. They did not think they could cope with a child permanently disabled in mind or body, and they definitely wanted to adopt rather than foster.

The society's social worker quickly realised that Martin and Cecilia were exceptionally intelligent caring people and that they were excellent parents to their sons. But since they could perfectly well have more babies if they wished, she did not think that giving the McCs a baby would be fair to the many childless couples on the society's list. And though she knew of several children under 5 who needed permanent substitute families, some of these youngsters had handicaps which the McCs would not have found acceptable. Others had parents in touch and were not free for adoption, or they were children whose early experiences had left them quite unable to cope with the competition inevitably offered by Martin and Cecilia's very bright, capable little boys. The social worker contacted other adoption agencies, but the story was the same. There was nothing for it but to suggest that this young couple wait until their boys were older and the age gap between them and a newcomer could be greater. She hoped very much that they would re-apply in a few years since they had so much to offer as parents, but she realised that by that time, from Martin and Cecilia's point of view, it might be too late.

Some families, however, never seem to think it is too late. They want to keep adding children even when all their resources are stretched to the limit. They appear to be 'child hungry', never satisfied. Bill and Martha were like that. They had two children by birth and two adopted as babies. Then they took three foster children. But still they wanted more. The staff in their local social services department were in a quandary. They needed good homes for their waiting children and in many respects Bill and Martha did offer a good home. Yet the social workers could see that it was in danger of becoming more like a small children's home than a real family.

Big families are fun and children can gain a lot from having several brothers and sisters. Some youngsters who have suffered many disappointments and disrupted relationships will do better in a very large household where close and intimate relationships can be avoided than in a small family where a deeply affectionate response is expected. But we now know from talking to children who have grown up in very large foster families that many of them felt there was never really enough time, love and attention to go round. There were just too many children, too much coming and going and the parents' personal resources of energy, interest and affection had to be spread too thinly. An important aspect of responsible parenthood is to know when enough is enough. Although some very large families are enormously successful, it is surely better to have one too few children than one too many.

OVERSEAS ORPHANS

Many people are attracted to the idea of offering a home to a destitute child from India, South America or the Far East. Every year wars, famines and earthquakes cause terrible havoc and distress. After each disaster, offers of homes pour into agencies like International Social Service or the Save the Children Fund. These offers can almost never be accepted. There are sound reasons why this should be so.

In many countries of the Third World as well as those hit by some natural or man-made calamity, children are hungry, diseased, homeless and sometimes orphaned. But this does not mean they are unwanted. Countries which have lost so much in the past through exploitation by richer Western nations, do not now wish to give away their children to be brought up by foreigners. Their children are their future.

Nor would rescuing even some thousands of needy children do anything really constructive to solve the child-care problems of the Third World. These peoples need education, medical care, clean water, better housing. Family feeling is strong in these communities and if financial help were available to families, few orphanages would be needed. It is almost always better to send money and experts to provide care on the spot than to try to arrange large scale inter-country adoption programmes.

Of course, there are occasional exceptions. Sometimes children of mixed parentage are not accepted by the community into which they were born. This happened to American servicemen's illegitimate children in Korea and Vietnam. In some cultures illegitimacy itself is such a disgrace that no unmarried mother can contemplate keeping her child with her. Individual children may also need long-term expensive medical care which is just not available in their own country, so to go overseas for adoption may be the only hope for certain youngsters.

A few children are brought into the United Kingdom for adoption each year, often by people who have lived or travelled abroad and have already adopted the child in his country of origin. It is, however, extremely complicated, time consuming and often expensive to bring a child to this country.

For all these reasons, adopting a foreign child is not really a practical possibility for the average couple seeking a baby or toddler to make their own.

## THE RESCUE MOTIVE

Most successful adoptions of 'special needs' children contain an element of the rescue motive and yet in too large doses it can prove disastrous. If you want to adopt because you have a strong urge to help a child in distress, you may find social workers are cautious about your motives and do not offer much encouragement. This is likely to make you angry and upset, but there are reasons for their caution. Here are some of them:

1    People who rescue a child are apt to expect gratitude. Not in words perhaps but in responsiveness, achievement, good behaviour and affection. Yet the child did not ask to be born or adopted and should not have to carry the burden of being grateful for what is a basic human right – the right to a family.

2    It often takes a child a very long time to recover from the experiences which made it necessary to rescue him. People who rescue may want quick results and will not always get them.

3    No one likes to be an object of pity. It makes one feel inferior. Being rescued may involve being pitied.

4    There is something romantic about the idea of rescuing a child, but being a parent is not romantic at all. It is a long hard slog, often up-hill.

5    Children who particularly need help often come with very unattractive habits. They are likely to whine, fight, tell lies, demand attention and wet their beds far more than the average child. Rescuers may not be prepared for this kind of reaction to their gallantry.

These are some of the dangerous, weak points of a rescue motive. There can be corresponding strengths that will weigh in the balance. Before you set out to adopt a child with any sort of handicap, you need to see how your own attitudes and capacities weigh in the scale.

If the overwhelming reason for applying to adopt is that you feel you 'ought', then stop right here and do not pursue the plan. Only go ahead if, in spite of some natural doubts and qualms, you genuinely want not only the challenge but the child.

# CHAPTER IV
# Childlessness

How much do you want to be a parent? This probably sounds a very silly question when everybody knows that you have been talking about wanting a baby for years. Sometimes, however, what we think we want and what we really want are not quite the same.

To be involuntarily childless can be one of life's great disappointments, but sometimes people really believe that they would like a child, while one part of their mind does not want to be a parent at all. Some young women secretly dread the responsibilities of motherhood and others are terrified of childbirth because of the exaggerated stories they have heard. There are men who do not really want to share their wife with a child or to have the responsibilities of a family. Sometimes one partner wants children and the other does not. If these conflicts are not resolved they will almost certainly lead to trouble and unhappiness, but their existence is often hidden even from the people concerned.

A fairly common situation is that of the Wright family. Natalie always spoke of her son Rupert's birth as having been exceptionally hard and difficult for her. She said that her husband would not let her go through such an ordeal again. It was never clear to her friends just why Mrs Wright's confinement had been so unusual, but they heard later that she had applied to adopt a child.

As the Wrights discussed their feelings and wishes with other couples waiting to adopt, it became rather obvious to everyone else that neither of them had any deep desire for parenthood. No specialist had advised against another pregnancy on medical grounds and there was no reason to suppose that because Natalie's first confinement had been hard her second would be the same. The truth was that she disliked being pregnant but felt that perhaps she should not let Rupert be an only child. Neither she nor her husband had stopped to think that adopting a child would bring its own problems. It seemed to them an easy way out of a difficulty.

INFERTILITY

If for more than a year you have been trying unsuccessfully to have children you should consult your family doctor. There may be some small thing wrong which can easily be corrected as there are a number of quite simple causes of diminished fertility. Perhaps your general health is not as good as it might be or the doctor may be able to give helpful advice about the sexual side of your marriage. On the other hand, it may be necessary for you to have a series of tests and examinations to try to discover the cause of your difficulty. In all cases, however, a really adequate physical examination is an essential first step in a serious consideration of adoption. Not everyone is willing to take this first step.

Sarah and Mat Smith were furious. The adoption agency to which they wanted to apply insisted that they have a physical examination to find out whether or not they could ever have a baby of their own. The Smiths were unwilling to do this and declared it was unnecessary red tape. The adoption agency felt that if this couple truly wanted a child they would have consulted a doctor long before this. The agency staff recognised that many people dislike medical examinations and that some busy infertility clinics can be rather insensitive to their patients' feelings, but they considered the Smiths' refusal to seek any medical help was a sign of immaturity and lack of any real desire for parenthood. If the Smiths did not truly want their own child why should they want to adopt one?

In about 50 per cent of cases of infertility, medical advice and treatment results in the longed for pregnancy. Like all the rest of us, doctors vary in their skills and interests and you may or may not find that yours is able and willing to give you time and help with this problem. The study of infertility is a relatively new science and fresh discoveries are made constantly. It is therefore almost always advisable to have the advice of a specialist if your own doctor's treatment does not have the desired results. He will very likely suggest this himself.

A good way to obtain the best possible advice or treatment for infertility is to join the National Association for the Childless (address at the end of this book). This excellent organisation offers information and guidance on fertility problems including lists of specialists and clinics and a network of individual counsellors and groups so that if you wish you can talk to people who are in a similar situation. Another possible source of information about treatment is your local marriage guidance council which is likely to be able to recommend a specialist in your area who is particularly interested in problems of infertility.

In many childless marriages both partners have some degree of infertility, but if it is the husband who is infertile and there is no reason why his wife should not conceive, artificial insemination is a possibility worth considering. Some people find it a distasteful idea or consider it morally wrong but there is an increasing number of couples turning to this method of achieving a family. If you are interested, you could find out more about it through your doctor or from the National Association for the Childless.

If you have been trying hard to conceive and have been undergoing a series of tests, the suggestions of the doctors may have increased your anxiety and upset your normal married life. It is easy to say 'stop worrying' but difficult to do. However, tension and stress can aggravate infertility, so you do have to try to find ways of relaxing. It might be a good idea to decide that for six months or a year you will stop trying so hard to get pregnant. If you have not conceived by the end of that time then you can start thinking seriously about alternatives, including adoption. It helps if you can have a holiday together and just enjoy one another's company. However much you may long for a baby there are lots of other things in life to enjoy while you are waiting, and this is a good time to make the most of them.

Sometimes a wife is willing to undergo any number of tests and try any suggested treatment, but her husband does not want to be examined. Some men refuse to consider the possibility that they may be the infertile partner. As they are physically healthy and able to have a satisfying sexual relationship they feel sure that the problem must lie with their wife. The whole idea seems new and strange to many people for it is not so very long since doctors discovered that husbands have problems of infertility nearly as often as their wives.

The Youngs were a couple like this. Mavis Young had been to every doctor and hospital in the area and had even had two minor operations, but still she did not become pregnant. The doctor wished to examine her husband but he refused. He was particularly opposed to the idea of having a specimen of his semen examined under a microscope. This is a very simple test which is almost always done if there is no obvious cause of infertility. Like many other men, Leslie Young was afraid that if it were discovered that he could not produce enough healthy sperm he would not be able to consider himself a real man.

It is easy to appreciate Leslie's feelings on the subject, but they are based on lack of knowledge. The glands which make a person virile and masculine are not the same ones that produce the sperm. As the people who work in sterility clinics know very well, it is quite often the athletes and 'he-men' who are sterile, while an apparently weak or effeminate man can father any number of children. Just because a man is infertile it does not mean that he is less brave and strong, less potent or less able to be a loving and dependable husband and father. We do not think that having a wrongly-shaped womb makes a woman less feminine and there is no reason to feel that a low sperm count makes a man less masculine. To learn that one cannot be a parent biologically is bound to be a blow to one's hopes, but it need not be a blow to one's self-respect. It can happen to anyone and there are many thousands of people in a similar situation. It may be that out of every ten couples one is involuntarily childless.

### YOUR FEELINGS ABOUT YOUR CHILDLESSNESS ARE VITALLY IMPORTANT

Perhaps you, too, are facing the disappointment of learning that you cannot have the children for which you planned. Or maybe you are in the almost more difficult situation where the doctors cannot find anything wrong and yet you still do not become pregnant. The prospect of remaining childless can be very hard to accept.

Most childless couples go through periods of great emotional distress, and feelings of anger, guilt, depression and worthlessness are very usual. To lose the hope of children is like a bereavement and yet it is more difficult to grieve than when one loses a known person through death because there is no focus for the grief. Nor do most childless couples receive sympathy and support from friends and relatives. Quite often indeed people's comments and questions are very hurtful, even when they do not mean them to be. Dealing with these intense feelings takes courage and time. When one is in the throes of pain or sorrow it seems as if it will never cease, but time really is a great healer and, in the end, most people can come to terms with hard realities. Though they do not stop minding, they become able to make other plans and get on with the important business of living. As one childless woman put it:

> My infertility resides in my heart as an old friend. I do not
> hear from it for weeks at a time, and then, a moment, a
> thought, a baby announcement or some such thing, and I will
> feel the tug - maybe even be sad or shed a few tears. And I
> think 'There's my old friend.' It will always be part of me.

All serious discussions about the success and failure of adoption placements are apt to come back again and again to the parents' feelings about their inability to have their own children. Until they can be comfortable about this, parents cannot be comfortable with an adopted child, for the child is a constant reminder of something they are trying to forget. This unresolved conflict will colour their attitudes towards the child, and may make them harsh and rejecting parents or over-protecting and spoiling. A situation of this sort disturbed the Brown family for years.

Brian was 'all boy' when Bill and Linda Brown adopted him. Even as a baby no one could have mistaken him for a little girl. He was a powerfully built child, noisy and clumsy sometimes but good-tempered and helpful and as devoted to his adopted mother as she was to him. With his father it was a different story. Somehow Bill never felt that Brian was really his son; the boy aggravated him with his loud, boisterous ways, but what riled him even more was the way Brian sided with his mother in any family argument and she in turn took his part. When people complimented him on his fine son, Bill never failed to mention that Brian was adopted. He tried to exert his authority by making arbitrary rules about the boy's activities and bedtime and insisting on unquestioning obedience even in trivial matters.

As Brian grew older the tension and rivalry between father and son grew until the boy took to staying out of the house as much as possible and hanging round with a group of friends. One day a newcomer to the neighbourhood suggested they 'borrow' a lorry and go for a ride. Always ready for fun, and angry over an argument with his father, Brian agreed to go along. There was the familiar story of the inexperienced driver, the stray dog and a fast car coming in the other direction. In the juvenile court Brian was put on probation for two years.

Fortunately, the probation officer was able to help not only Brian but his parents too. He saw the family regularly and as the weeks went by they came to like and trust him. For the first time, Bill was able to discuss some of the deep feelings and fears which he had tried to hide even from himself. With the probation officer's help he was gradually able to realise that he had never got over the shock of learning that he was sterile and could never father a child. The fact that his sterility was caused by a severe attack of mumps when he was a boy did not prevent his feeling less than a whole man. He had never told a soul except his wife and they had allowed their families and friends to think it was his wife who could not conceive. When Linda suggested adoption he was not too keen on the idea but she was so anxious for a child that he had felt mean to refuse his consent. He thought he might have liked a little girl but when they were offered a bouncing boy Linda's joy was so great that he had pretended an enthusiasm that he did not feel and hoped he would learn to love the child later.

It was a pity for all of them that Brian was such a masculine youngster. The irritation that Bill felt when he looked at him was explained by his feelings of inferiority – his jealousy of his son's exuberant vitality. Bill Brown was a good football player himself and if this had been his own son he would have gloried in Brian's athletic ability and been proud when people remarked on their resemblance to one another. He would have been glad to see the boy's affection for his mother. But as it was, he had felt all these things as a threat. Unconsciously, he had looked on his son as a rival for his wife's affection.

It was only as he came to understand these feelings and accept them that Bill Brown regained his self-confidence and was able to enjoy the role of father without the need to dominate and bluster.

DO YOU BOTH WANT A CHILD?

It quite often happens that to begin with one marriage partner is more keen on adoption than the other. Sometimes it is the husband who first suggests it, but more often it is the wife. Generally the enthusiasm of one arouses the interest of the other so that before they take a child into their home both husband and wife are full of happy expectations. Sometimes, however, one or the other of them really does not want to adopt. People who love each other naturally want to please one another, but it is no kindness to agree to adoption if you are uncertain about it, let alone if you genuinely dislike the idea.

Not all fathers especially enjoy the bottle-and-nappy stage of their children's lives, though nowadays many of them are experts in baby care and love it. The fact that the man does not long for a baby in the house is not vitally important if he truly wants an adopted family and is able to accept an adopted child as his own.

Not every woman longs to care for an infant. Some mothers are much better with older children. In these cases, adopting a school-age child may be the ideal solution. But since the main work of caring for children is still done by the mother in most families, it is vitally important that the wife should really want to take on this responsibility and not do it just because she feels sorry that she has been unable to give her husband a child. 'George always wanted a son so much,' Joyce explained to the social worker at the child guidance clinic, 'but I never thought he'd pick one that was as much trouble as this.' She went on to say that she had never felt well since their adopted son entered their home. The broken nights and extra work had been too much for her when he was a baby and now she found an over-active, difficult 5-year-old almost more than she could stand. The youngster was a model child with his daddy, but alone with her he was a constant nuisance, disobedient and destructive. She blamed this on his heredity and had never thought that the little boy, sensing her rejection and unwillingness to be a mother to him, had responded with anger and bad behaviour.

How can you make certain that your husband or wife is not just agreeing to adoption to please you? One way is to make sure that you both carry some responsibility for making the arrangements. It is not what a person says, but what he feels, that counts here. What he feels can sometimes be deduced from how he acts. When a husband finds that he has to write all the letters to the adoption agency, make the phone calls and fill out all the forms, or a wife finds that her husband is always too busy to come with her for an interview, then there is a possibility that both marriage partners are not equally ready to go forward. Of course this is not an infallible rule, but it can be a guide.

# CHAPTER V

# Some important points to consider

The last two chapters have explained some of the factors people need to consider in deciding whether they want to be parents. You might think that ought to be enough self-probing and heart-searching – you might well think so but it would not be true! It is hard to delve into hidden feelings and bring them up into the light for examination, but with such an important issue at stake we need to be as thorough and objective as possible. It is not just a question of whether an adoption agency will accept your application, though obviously that is important. Of much more fundamental importance is to consider whether adopting a child is the right plan for you and, if so, what sort of child.

Before you finally decide, look again at yourselves, the foundation stones of the new family you hope to build. Look at your life-style and the changes adopting would bring. Look too at the worries and difficulties which all parents must expect in bringing up their children. Even if you are planning to adopt a baby, rather than an older child, be realistic about the possibility that you may have to face a few more problems just because yours will be an adopted family and because you will need to meet them with a little extra wisdom and sensitive understanding.

Of course you will not be perfect parents, nobody is and fortunately, perfection is not necessary. You cannot hope to foresee all the pleasures of a family or all the big and little crises that will arise. It is possible, however, to have a fairly good idea of what is involved and whether you have at least a good average chance of success. You can most likely offer a child a loving and secure home with adequate food and shelter and plenty of laughter, a home where he can experience the give and take of family life and develop his potentialities to the full. But some couples do have the scales weighted against them on account of their age, their 'nerves' or their unrealistic expectations of children.

## YOUR AGE

The only legal specification as to the age of the adopters is that both must be over 21. Most adoption agencies, however, do not place babies with couples who are above child-bearing age, indeed the limit may be set at 35 or even lower. This may seem unfair and arbitrary. Rules like that are made partly because of the practical necessity to keep the number of applications within bounds but there are genuine grounds for concern about adoptive parents' age.

When a child is placed the agency is not only considering the present but also looking into the future. Most women of 45 are quite capable of looking after an infant even if they do find the broken nights and constant washing rather tiring. Not so many of them at 55 or 60 have the energy and patience to cope with the tiresome ways of a teenage son or daughter. Even when they feel young, fathers and mothers past middle age are less likely to want to share their children's interests and activities. What is worse, adolescent children may look upon their elderly parents as 'old fogies' who could not possibly understand how they feel about the latest boy friend or a burning interest in science which absolutely necessitates turning the garden shed into an experimental laboratory! It may not be true that older parents are unable to understand these needs and aspirations but it is a fact that such couples are working against nature. They could well be less flexible, more easily tired and irritable and less a part of their children's lives.

It is the age gap between parent and child that matters. So though you may be considered too old for a baby, you could be just the right age to become the parent of a school-age child. Your friends' children are probably in that age group too. Older couples who have brought up a family may have a wealth of wisdom and experience to offer as parents to a troubled teenager and there are many, many youngsters of this age waiting for a foster or adoptive home.

People applying for a handicapped child may find that age barriers are lifted. Agencies have to be realistic on behalf of children. It is best for babies to have young parents but better to have older parents than none at all. So for children for whom homes are scarce, some of the usual rules may quite properly be set aside.

## CHANGING PATTERNS OF LIVING

A very real consideration for childless couples is the fundamental change that children will bring to their way of life. All new parents are called upon to make adjustments in their ways but this is harder to do if you have had an established routine and pattern of living for many years.

Sometimes an ambitious couple will decide that before starting a family they will work and save for a comfortable home of their own. Julia and John Briggs thought this way. John Briggs was a successful insurance agent and his wife was a secretary. Gradually they saved enough to buy a charming, modern bungalow, attractive furniture and a good car. They were happy together and enjoyed their well-planned lives and comfortable home.

When Julia was 38 and John nearly 40 they had all the things they needed and felt ready to start a family – but no babies came. After a while they consulted their doctor and several specialists who told them that their peak period of fertility and the years when they could most likely have had a baby were past. In great distress they applied to several adoption agencies but none was able to place a child with them. The Briggs were used to being able to have whatever they wanted and had worked for, so they took this disappointment very badly.

A year or two later, a friend told them about a young woman who wanted to place her 2-year-old son, Harry, for adoption. Her husband had deserted her and she planned to remarry but her new boyfriend did not want the child. Harry was a good-looking little fellow but his behaviour was far from attractive. His mother had given him little love and less training, but he bitterly resented this new mummy and daddy who had all sorts of strange rules about what he must and must not do. He was dirty, destructive and very unhappy. In a few weeks the Briggs' beautiful bungalow was showing sad signs of wear and tear and Julia was worn out with trying to comfort and amuse him. When John came home at night she was tired and cross and often the supper was unprepared. None of this fitted in with their plans for family life and though they felt very badly about the whole experience, they decided to return Harry to his mother. Unfortunately, she had left town and could not be found, and it was some time before the Briggs were able to place Harry with a children's society who could care for him and find him a more suitable permanent home.

In many ways, of course, adding a school-age child to the household is less disruptive of routines than a baby, yet any new member of a family will mean change and adjustment and extra work. Though older children do not require 6 a.m. bottles and nappy changes, they do have nightmares and tantrums, wet their beds and need help with their homework when you may want to relax. They also stay up much later. People who adopt an older child often find that one of the hardest things is not having the evening to themselves and not having much chance to talk to each other without the child being present.

### HOW GOOD IS YOUR HEALTH?

Besides your age you will want to give some thought to your health. Both for your own sake and for that of the child you certainly should try to make sure that you are in good health, can take on extra work and responsibility and have a normal expectation of life. You will want to find out these things before you take a child into your home, since if you wait until the time of the actual adoption proceedings, you and the child will already have become part of one another's lives. The court hearing your adoption application will want to know about your physical and mental health, and should any medical reasons against the adoption be discovered at that late date you and the child will all suffer.

Even more important than your physical health are your temperament and emotional stamina. Are you 'the anxious type', always expecting the worst, or are you even-tempered and generally cheerful? When a crisis occurs do you have to take to your bed with a sick headache or can you start working to find a solution? Do you suffer from stomach ulcers or nervous indigestion or frequently have to consult the doctor for your nerves? Has either of you ever had any form of nervous breakdown?

It is generally unwise to make dogmatic statements about adoption since some of the most unlikely placements have worked out happily and the reverse is occasionally true. However, it can be stated quite definitely that no one who is having a nervous breakdown should adopt a child and anyone who has had such a breakdown in the past should seek professional advice before planning adoption. Those who have rather more than they can manage in running their own lives and keeping on an even keel are not likely to have the emotional strength to bring up an adopted family.

It is a sad indication of our lack of understanding of children's needs and the challenge they present, that people sometimes recommend adoption as a cure for the neurotic and even the mentally ill. Sometimes bearing a child will help a nervy or self-centred woman to forget herself and her troubles for a time, but adoption is another matter and those who recommend it to such a woman cannot have appreciated the almost certain unhappiness for everyone concerned.

## SINGLE PARENTS

When legal adoption first started, there were quite a lot of adoptions by single women. Then for a period most agencies insisted on placing babies with married couples. They felt that, as many unmarried mothers were giving up their babies so as to provide the child with the advantage of having a father, it seemed foolish and contrary to the mother's wishes to accept a baby from one single woman and give it to another.

The changing pattern of adoption has led to real changes in agency attitudes. While it is most unlikely that a healthy infant would be placed with a single adopter, an increasing number of agencies will now consider applications from a single man or woman to adopt an older child or a handicapped baby. Some children who have had a particularly close or a particularly difficult relationship with one of their original parents, can do better with a single adoptive parent of the opposite sex. Some severely handicapped children benefit from the intensity of devotion that perhaps only a single parent can give.

Maureen Connolly had a nursing training and worked in a special home for mentally and physically handicapped children. She was good at her job and found it satisfying in many ways, but she longed for a child of her own and had a strong religious belief that God's plan for her life was that she should become mother to a severely handicapped child. The first two societies she applied to would not consider her seriously. They thought she was rather odd and would never be able to cope. Then she found an agency that specialised in placing children with problems of one sort or another. Here she got a very different reception. In the end a small miracle occurred. Maureen adopted Paul who is both blind and mentally handicapped. On the hospital ward in which he had previously lived with twenty-five other handicapped children,

Paul did not respond much to anyone. He just rocked himself to and fro and made strange noises in his throat. Now his loving relationship with Maureen is a joy to see.

Maureen would be the first to acknowledge that she could not have achieved this without a lot of help from her family and friends. To bring up a child successfully, a single person must have back-up support, not only for emergencies when the parent is ill, but also help with more everyday care. No one can be a good parent every minute of every day without relief and children need a circle of adults who care about them, not a narrow or possessive relationship with one person.

Ben Jocelyn had difficulty in achieving adoption. He was an electrician and first met Roger (12) and Tommy (9) when he was doing some work in their children's home known as The Gables. The job lasted quite a few weeks and during this time Ben discovered that Roger shared his passion for fishing. One Saturday he invited the boy to go with him. The staff at The Gables were a little dubious because Roger was known to be obstreperous and difficult to handle, but the expedition was a great success. Ben started taking Roger out quite regularly for fishing or to football matches or a meal at his home, and he also came to The Gables and played with all the children. He got to know Tommy too. The three enjoyed each other's company and it became increasingly difficult to say goodbye when it came time for Ben to leave or the boys to go back to the home.

It was Ben's sister who said: 'Why don't you adopt them?' After a lot of thought he determined to try even though he was not at all sure that the social services department responsible for the boys would agree to their being adopted by a single man. Ben's marriage had broken up after two unhappy years and there had been no children. At that time he was in the Navy and decided against marrying again while he was still going to sea. He left the service when he was in his mid-30s, bought a little house near his parents and just assumed he would meet a nice girl and marry again. But somehow his friendships never deepened into marriage and he became rather used to his bachelor life. The one thing he really missed was children. He saw a lot of his nephews and nieces but naturally they were often taken up with their own family doings.

The staff in the social services department were indeed very doubtful at first. They had never placed a child for adoption with a single man. Some people questioned his motives and others wondered how he would ever manage the practical problems of supervision for the boys after school, during holidays or if they were ill.

Fortunately Ben was a very mature, stable, patient and persistent person. He put his case persuasively, tolerated an exceptionally long series of meetings and interviews, had the full backing and promise of help from his family and neighbours and gradually persuaded the social workers and the social services department's adoption committee to agree to the placement. In all of this he was greatly helped by the support of the staff at The Gables. They were sure that having Ben as a father was just what Roger and Tommy needed and they could report on the enormous improvement in the boys' happiness and behaviour since Ben became part of their lives.

There were the usual settling-in problems. Roger and Tommy tested Ben to the limits of his energy and patience and created strains in his relationship with his family who also suffered from the boys' bad behaviour at times. There were days when Ben looked back with nostalgia to his quiet evenings at home or the chance to go down to the pub for a pint and game of darts. But he never really regretted becoming a father and when the social workers saw the improvement in adjustment and school work that both boys showed at the end of their first year with Ben, they were more than satisfied to recommend to the court that an adoption order be granted.

## WORKING MOTHERS

Many people hold strong views about the pros and cons of mothers working outside the home. Recent studies have shown that mothers often benefit from the change of scene and adult companionship that a job provides and that most children do not suffer if the substitute care is good enough.

Some people are fortunate enough to have a relative or close friend who is able and willing to act as a regular substitute mother. Others live near to a day nursery or good after-school play centre. But for many mothers the finding of suitable caretakers for school holidays, after school or when a child is ill becomes a constant worry and the strain of a full-time job and being mother, wife and housewife can be almost unbearable at times. Part-time work is, of course, much easier to manage even if difficult to obtain. It is often very beneficial all round, especially when the baby has reached the age of 2 + and can begin to enjoy the companionship of other children.

There are some special points in regard to adopted children and working mothers which need to be taken into consideration. Adopted children and their parents need to grow together. The bond which normally ties a mother to the baby she has carried and borne is lacking at first in the adoption situation. A bond that is equally strong can, and does, grow as the mother and father feed and care for their adopted child, learn to understand his wants and anticipate his needs. It grows as the baby learns that those who give him love and attention are his parents. Babies can only recognise love as it comes to them through physical care and attention, so those who immediately give their adopted baby into the full-time care of another person run the risk of losing something very precious. Perhaps, too, they do not want to be mothers as much as they think they do.

Opportunities for the development of close parent-child bonds are also important when an older child is being adopted. Just because the early years have been lost, parents need to make use of all the available time to build up the relationship. The period when a child first gets in from school is often one of those times. Not only does the child want to share the pleasures and tribulations of the day, the picture he drew, the star for sums or the trouble in the playground. He may also need the security of having his mother or father at home and waiting for him. Children who have lost important adults in the past live in constant if unspoken dread of losing their new parents too. To arrive home to an unexpectedly empty house can cause panic. On the other hand, returning home to a warm welcome, a snack and a chance for a quiet moment for talk before going out to play can be an important factor in developing trust and communication within the family.

Most adoption agencies will want to be sure that an adoptive mother plans to stay home with a new baby for at least six months after placement and that she can arrange really satisfactory care if she goes back to work after that. But in special circumstances exceptions to rules can always be made. So if you must work but can make satisfactory child care arrangements, do not be afraid to press your case.

YOUR FINANCIAL SITUATION

Amid the keen competition for the babies available for adoption some unsuccessful couples may think that families with wealth and influence have been favoured and given priority. It is not true that having a large bank balance will take you to the head of the queue. A good adoption agency is concerned to find the right home for each child in its care, not the richest or grandest but the home which will suit that particular child. The social workers need to know that an adoptive family can manage on its income whatever that income may be. They will want to know that your home is at least reasonably well kept and that you have sufficient space so that the child can have a bed of his own and a bedroom either to himself or with another child of the same sex.

But beyond these basic, minimum requirements money and houses are unimportant compared with a child's need for love, security and a sense of belonging. A farm labourer and his wife may be just as acceptable adopters as wealthy landowners and the foreman of a factory may be more likely to get a child than the managing director.

If you would like more children, can consider a 'special needs' child but feel you cannot afford to add another through adoption, or if you are a single parent or interested in adopting a family group of two or three brothers and sisters, it is worth inquiring about the possibility of an adoption allowance or about attendance and mobility allowances for handicapped children. Or you might consider long-term fostering. The various allowances may not cover the whole cost of bringing up a child but they will help a great deal and might make it possible for you to have a much larger family than you had dared to hope for. A single adoptive parent is entitled to register for social security payment and need not register for work while the child is of school age.

LOCAL RESOURCES FOR THE HANDICAPPED

Anyone who is considering whether to take a disabled child into the family will need to investigate local resources for education and medical care. Your child may need to attend a special class in an ordinary school or even a special school. Is there such a class or school within easy reach and would a place be available? Would your doctor be sympathetic and interested? What about transport for hospital appointments or physiotherapy? Is your house suitable for a wheelchair or can it be adapted if necessary? Are there local resources for respite care if you should become ill or urgently need a break? These are just some of the practical questions to which you will need answers.

Obviously you cannot explore every possibility for every sort of handicap but your plans might be influenced by discovering for instance that there is an excellent class for deaf children in your local school but that the nearest school for the educationally sub-normal is on the far side of town and always has a long waiting list. Or you might learn to your surprise that the relatives on whom you would most depend for help would feel unable to care for a child who had epileptic seizures or that they fear their own children would be distressed by any kind of physical deformity. There might be a particularly helpful local group for families of children with Down's Syndrome or an excellent indoor pool for a child who needs to swim as part of his therapy. These are the sort of things that you will want to find out about before you decide what sort of child you could parent most successfully and enjoyably.

Local resources really are important because however much you do at home, you and your handicapped child will need to depend quite a bit on the help available in your local community. One of the points to think about if you are considering adopting an older or handicapped child, is whether you are a very private family or whether you are happy to accept help from outside experts. Some people find it difficult to have outsiders involved in their family affairs.

YOUR OWN CHILDREN'S NEEDS

All responsible parents give careful thought to their existing children when they contemplate having another child. There are the obvious things like money and bedroom space and the more subtle things like the most appropriate age gap. If the newcomer is joining the family through adoption or fostering, you will have more choice and control over some things and less over others.

A brand new baby may not impinge much on the lives of older brothers and sisters. A baby may take up mother's time, but it does not get into older children's bedrooms, break up their toys or tear their books. A baby does not want to share games or friends, it does not tell tales or pinch and kick under the table as an older child can do. If you add an older child to the family, your existing children will almost certainly have to make a lot of adjustments from the very first day onward and the success of the venture will depend a great deal on how well they can cope with the demands and pressures that these adjustments will inevitably impose. Most families who have gone through this experience feel that they have all gained a great deal from it. However there are costs to be counted too.

The costs may be particularly high if the newcomer is handicapped either mentally or physically. Having one disabled member can handicap a whole family in some respects while enlarging their horizons in others. Outings may have to be curtailed and choice of holidays limited; other children may tease or shun. Children can feel overly responsible for a handicapped brother or sister and their own social life may suffer as a result. Certainly prospective adopters of a handicapped child should not expect their other youngsters to give up too much or they will naturally come to resent the demands made upon them. Nor should they automatically be expected to assume the responsibility of caring for the disabled member of the family when parents are no longer able to do so.

## WHAT SORT OF CHILDREN DO YOU LIKE?

Most people, when asked, will say that they like children, but on closer investigation this liking is very varied. At one end of the scale are those who are not really happy unless they have a child or two around. These are the couples who borrow children to take with them on expeditions and picnics, the people who run cub packs or mind the babies during church services. At the other end of the scale are those who enjoy having a well-behaved child to spend a few hours or even a week-end in their otherwise adult-centred home. Where on the scale do you come?

What kind of children do you enjoy most and what is it about the others that you find trying? Do you like most of the children you meet, not only your relatives but the noisy little boys next door or the school children you see on the bus every morning? Or do you find yourselves criticising the way these youngsters behave and feeling that if you were bringing them up they would behave better? It is as well to face realities here. It is not really too likely that the child you bring up will be different, and when you get down to it, why should you want him to be?

If you find that you want a child who will differ a lot from the others in the neighbourhood maybe you do not truly want a child at all. The woman who wants a pretty little girl just because she likes to sew and make pretty dresses does not really want a flesh-and-blood child. This does not mean that mothers should not enjoy dressing their daughters attractively – every proud mother does. It is just that this reason alone is not solid enough to stand up to the pressures as well as the pleasures of bringing up a child. Unfortunately people have sometimes taken a child as a plaything when they would have done better to buy a pet or join a golf club.

If you have not had the opportunity to get to know many children and teenagers, it will be more difficult for you to know whether you will enjoy having them twenty-four hours a day and seven days a week. It is a great help if you can get some first-hand experience with children before you finally decide about adoption. You can probably baby-sit for your neighbours or mind their children while they go shopping. You can invite the children of your friends and relatives to spend days or holidays with you or perhaps give a helping hand to some underprivileged child in your neighbourhood.

Another excellent way to find out what children and adolescents are really like is to help with a scout, guide or cub pack or your local youth club. If none exists, perhaps you could start one. This will not only be a constructive community service but it will also give you knowledge of a variety of children and how successful you are in handling them. Do not be discouraged, though, if your first efforts are not entirely successful. Everyone has to learn to be a parent or a club leader and everyone makes mistakes along the way. You are bound to have some difficulties, especially when you are dealing with more or less unknown children.

If you are thinking of taking on a disabled child or a baby with Down's Syndrome, you should definitely make a point of meeting youngsters with the same sort of handicap. You will want to talk to their parents and find out what is really involved in the care of such a child, what it will demand of you, how the problems change as the child grows older, and what sort of help you will need. Your local health visitor can possibly suggest one or two families you could visit. You may be able to visit some schools or clubs for handicapped youngsters. Your local citizens advice bureau, health department or social services department will almost certainly be able to tell you about local groups of parents of handicapped children. You will probably find them very friendly, welcoming and anxious to be of help, but they might find it difficult at first to believe that you are deliberately planning to care for a disabled child.

One of the advantages of adopting an older child is that you can know a lot more about him than about a baby. There is less likelihood that you will unwittingly find yourself bringing up a child whose whole temperament is just so different from your own that you always have trouble understanding each other. This can happen when one adopts a baby, just as it can when children are born into a family.

Agencies placing older children for adoption or long-term fostering try very hard to suggest combinations of parents and child that are likely to be mutually compatible. But if they are to do this satisfactorily, you will need to explain what is most important to you about a child's character, what your expectations are and what sorts of behaviour you find it particularly hard to tolerate. You must study yourself as well as the child. Some of the questions you might ask yourself are:

1  Do I like children to be very affectionate and cuddly or am I a bit undemonstrative myself?
2  How much would a child's school achievement and exam results matter to me? Are my expectations for a child really just ordinary or do I hope for a youngster who is actually better than average academically, who will get not just CSEs but A levels, who will enjoy music and books and good conversation and go on to a successful career in business or one of the professions?
3  Do I prefer the sort of child who yells and kicks and has tantrums or one who is moody and silent when he is upset? Can I cope better with aggression or with fears and phobias?
4  Can I tolerate whiny, babyish behaviour from a child old enough to know better or pseudo maturity from a youngster who has had to grow up too quickly?
5  Are we a family that likes to share all our interests and activities or do we happily go our separate ways?
6  Do I hope for a child who is keen on all sorts of hobbies, sports and activities or do I remember with sympathy my own times hanging round the neighbourhood with a group of friends or holed-up in my bedroom watching TV or reading magazines?
7  What would 'get my goat' worst, lies, wet beds, stealing, carelessness, indifference or cheating?
8  What do I most look forward to about having a child (or another child) in our home?

## WHITE PARENTS AND BLACK CHILDREN

If you are white and are considering adopting a black child, there are a number of things you need to think about very carefully.

You need to face the reality that to all intents and purposes you are going to become a black family with all that this implies about being on the receiving end of racial prejudice in a social situation. People are going to stare at you. Many will make the assumption that the black member of the family is the wife's illegitimate child. Many adopters have said that they are aware of this by the way people react on the street. Will you be able to put up with this? Getting angry and upset will neither help anyone nor stop it happening.

It is no good just saying that colour is not important to you. It is important to people in general. While adoptive families do genuinely forget that their black children are different, the world outside does not forget and even mixed race children are looked upon as black. This can create some special problems for them if they have been brought up in an all-white family and community and have come to think of themselves as white.

Just because they themselves never think about it, loving parents can all too easily deny their child the opportunity of seeing himself as black. This is why adopters have to take positive steps to enable their child to identify with his own people's culture and history. Are you prepared to take trouble to learn about these things? Unfortunately, you cannot rely on television and the press to provide a good and positive image of black people. All too often they are represented as troublesome, inadequate or inarticulate and this will not help a child feel proud of being black. An adoptive mother told how her little black daughter was chosen to be the princess in her school play but came home saying wistfully, 'But you can't really have black princesses, can you Mummy?' Clearly, this child needed someone to teach her some of the history of splendid black civilisations.

Much the best way for white adoptive parents to give their child comfort and pride in his colour is for them to have some black friends. Showing that you admire and respect as well as like them will encourage your child to identify with confident and successful black people.

Perhaps the most difficult part of adopting across racial lines is that it makes one realise how racially prejudiced we really are even though we think we are tolerant and accepting. However much we may feel that we have not responded to the racial stereotypes presented to us, the process is insidious. Like the constant drip, drip of a tap, the ideas and preconceived notions are fed to us bit by bit and we are usually unaware of the process.

Becoming the parent of a black child makes one suddenly aware of one's own prejudices as well as those of other people. Since most of us do not admit to prejudice and do not like to talk about it, becoming aware of one's own unacceptable feelings can be a lonely and uncomfortable process.

On the positive side of the trans-racial adoption experience is the real acceptance by black people that the mixed family can enjoy. The demonstration that you are not racially prejudiced will make black people's attitude to you quite different. A white woman who cared for a black teenager for several years described this experience as being quite stunning. She says that she, too, saw black people in a new light and it was a heartwarming experience to be received as one of them.

## TAKING YOUR TIME

So many questions, so many uncomfortable possibilities and such far-reaching decisions to be taken, how can you ever sort out all these perplexing problems? How can you be sure when you are truly ready to adopt a child?

Some people are lucky enough to know without doubt that if they cannot have a family by birth they want to have one by adoption. Most, however, reach this point slowly and sometimes painfully. Quite often well-meaning doctors or friends will advise a couple who have lost a baby or learned that they cannot have one to go right out and try to adopt one. This advice, though given in all good faith, is most unwise. No one who is suffering from shock and grief is in a fit state to make an important long-term decision. Even people who are not under any particular strain are generally advised to go home and think about it for a few days before deciding whether to take a new job, move house or buy an expensive piece of furniture. How much more important to take time over making a decision that will affect every aspect of your lives and the whole future of a child.

Time is, in fact, essential in a sound plan, whether you are hoping for a traditional baby adoption or the very different undertaking of adopting an older child. Some people recover rather quickly from a shock and do not have too much difficulty in adjusting to new situations. For others it may take weeks and months before they can even face up to the fact that they will not be able to produce a baby in the way their friends do. Most of us have to live with unpalatable facts for a while before we get used to them and can gradually accept them. A period of mourning for a lost baby is natural and necessary. At first perhaps you can hardly bear to see your neighbour with her baby in her arms, but later you will be able to look at that baby and other children around you and think whether you would enjoy having them for your own. At first you may find it hard to talk of your disappointment and what it means, even to each other, but gradually you should be able to share all your hurt and angry feelings and plan together for the future.

Each husband and wife will need to work out these problems for themselves and in their own time. But maybe, while you are thinking, these guidelines will help you to determine when you are ready to go ahead in the adventure of adoption.

1   Have you satisfied yourselves that medical science cannot help you to have your own child?

2   Is your marriage built on mutual love and trust and can you share your thoughts, problems and pleasures? Is your relationship strong enough to withstand the extra pressures of adoptive parenthood?

3   Do you both have a sincere desire and longing for parenthood? Are you agreed about the sort of child you want and the way to bring him up?

4   Are you able to discuss adoption plans not only with one another but with your families and close friends? As you do this, does it seem to you an acceptable and happy way to build a family or do you think of it always as a second best?

5   Can you tolerate it if some of your relatives and friends do not understand your wish to bring a black or handicapped youngster into the family?

6   Have you taken the trouble to find out whether you really like having children about the house when they are naughty as well as when they are good?

7   If you are planning to take an older or disabled child, have you honestly faced what could be involved? Can you accept outside help when this is needed?

8   Do you feel comfortable about your willingness and ability to weather the work, the anxieties and the big and little crises that are an inevitable part of family life? Do you believe that you can offer a warm, secure home in which children can grow up to be themselves even if this is rather different from what you hoped or expected?

If you cannot honestly answer yes to these questions it may be that adoption is not for you and that your future happiness lies along another path. Or it could be that you just need more time to get used to the idea and perhaps an opportunity to talk things over with someone who understands the problems involved.

# CHAPTER VI

# Alternatives to adoption

As there are so few available babies compared with the number of people who want them, very many would-be adopters are bound to be disappointed. Although you have a wonderful home to offer there may be no baby for you. It could well be, therefore, that in spite of your desire for parenthood you will have to find some other way to satisfy the longing in your hearts and occupy the time on your hands.

Or perhaps, for good reasons, you have decided against taking on the long-term responsibility of an adopted family but you would like to find some way of helping children and having them as part of your life.

In either case you will want to consider the alternatives. Even though these alternatives do not seem so satisfying it does not mean that they are not worth considering. It is foolish to say that because one cannot have exactly what one wants then one will not have anything at all. There are thousands of children needing help and affection; some are lonely and unloved, some are handicapped in mind or body, others live in overcrowded squalor. You can be a friend to children even if you cannot be a parent. Perhaps you can help some individual child towards a happier life or can work for improved conditions for whole groups of youngsters. Community service of this kind can bring you deep rewards and satisfactions and your help is very much needed.

## FOSTER CHILDREN

Taking a foster child to board in your home is the most obvious alternative to adoption. There are many kinds of fostering and it is really very important that anyone thinking of becoming a foster parent should understand the differences.

There are four main categories of foster care so it may help to say a little about each in turn. But before doing so we need to refer once more to that rather confusing term 'fostering with a view to adoption'. This is not really fostering in the true sense. It is not an alternative to adoption but a method of achieving it. As we have seen in previous chapters, there are various reasons why a child for whom adoption is the plan, may have to be placed with his new family on a fostering basis in the first instance. In these cases however the goal is clearly adoption even if this is expected to take a long time and there are risks along the way.

*Short-stay fostering*
Short-stay foster homes are mainly used to help in family emergencies. The need could arise from something very straight-forward like a mother going to hospital for an operation or confinement when no relatives are available to care for the other children. It could be much more complicated like a young mother at the end of her tether and in danger of abusing her baby, or a teenager so badly at odds with his parents that they all need a cooling-off period.

Being a short-stay foster parent is not easy but it is a deeply interesting and rewarding occupation. Often it involves the foster parents in work with the child's whole family. Wherever possible, parents are encouraged to visit and keep in close touch; otherwise the child feels deserted and when he goes home his parents seem like strangers. There must also be a real working partnership between social workers and foster parents on behalf of the child and his family.

*Professional fostering*
Many local authorities now have what are known as 'professional' fostering schemes. The objective is to provide family care rather than institutional care for children or young people with serious problems. The majority are adolescents but some are younger children with major mental or physical handicaps.

Professional foster parents are paid a salary over and above the normal boarding out rates and in return they contract to care for the child, usually for a specified length of time. They are usually expected to attend special training courses and take part in regular support and discussion groups. Such foster parents become somewhat like home-based staff members.

*Long-stay fostering*
A foster placement that lasts more than six months is usually considered long-stay. More often than not, the length of stay will be rather uncertain when the child is first placed. The objective is to provide loving care in a family setting until the child can return to his own parents or live independently. The parents may be having marriage problems or be temporarily homeless. The mother may be in a mental hospital or father in prison. A teenager may be unable to get along at home and need a foster family that can provide a bridge to independent adult living. There are so many problems and tragedies that can lead to children coming into public care and needing substitute families for a while.

Long-stay fostering avoids the constant change and partings that are inevitable in short-stay arrangements, but it, too, is a partnership. Foster parents usually have to share the child with his own family who will usually, but not always, be encouraged to visit and keep in touch, and also with the agency which placed the child. There can be both advantages and disadvantages about this sort of sharing. The disadvantages may be lack of security or the need to refer major decisions to the local authority or voluntary society which placed the child and which retains final responsibility. The advantages are in the financial and moral support which the agency and its social workers can offer. Not all social workers are equally competent, experienced and congenial, but as one experienced foster mother put it: 'Having a good social worker behind you is half the battle.'

Various problems can arise in the day-to-day and year-by-year care of a foster child. Many of these youngsters have been scarred by earlier experiences and are quite disturbed and difficult to manage. Some have health problems or are mentally retarded. Sometimes they are deeply torn in their loyalty and have great difficulty coping with the realities and the fantasies that arise from having two sets of parents. Sometimes the relationships between foster parents and the child's own parents are also strained. And, of course, when the day comes for the child to return home it is hard for foster parents to say goodbye without clinging and to take an unselfish pleasure in having helped put the family together again. The support of a knowledgeable and sympathetic social worker can be a great help in all these situations, for a problem shared is half cured. Other foster parents are also likely to be a great help, and in most areas there are now groups of foster parents linked with the National Foster Care Association. Attending their meetings or talking to members can be an excellent way of finding out more about what is involved.

*Permanent fostering*
It is of the essence of foster care that nothing is 100 per cent certain and permanence can never be guaranteed, but there are some children for whom return home seems impossible and for whom adoption is either impractical or undesirable. Lisa and Marlene had been in care on a number of occasions before they went to live with the Neville family. Their parents were divorced and their father had moved to another part of the country where he had a new wife and several children. Their mother had a series of admissions to mental hospital and the doctors now said that she would never again be well enough to look after the girls. Lisa and Marlene had not much liked living in a children's home and were eager to become part of the Neville household and share the happy family life they found there, but they remained very fond of their mother, liked to visit her when she was well enough and also wanted to keep contact with their grandmother and an aunt who loved the girls but could not offer them a home. Nor did they want to change their names. Everyone understood that placement with the Nevilles was intended to last until the girls grew up and left home, as they would in any family, but adoption would have been inappropriate.

There are some families who can offer total security and commitment to a child but who need the financial help of a boarding-out allowance. Permanent fostering can provide the opportunity for parents with large hearts and small incomes to have a big family.

It does sometimes happen that a child originally placed for fostering becomes available for adoption, but this is not something anyone should count on. If you really want a child for your very own and do not feel able to share him with his original family or the agency, it would be a bad mistake to become foster parents unless the plan is quite definitely eventual adoption and you have a clear agreement with the agency about this. Caught between foster parents who want to possess him and original parents who do not want to give him up, the unfortunate child can become the victim of an emotional tug-of-war.

Nevertheless, fostering is often a genuine alternative to adoption. Not everyone can do this exacting job but many men and women find it wonderfully rewarding work. Foster children need a great deal of attention and affection and frequently they have little to give back. The most successful foster parents are generally those who have plenty of other satisfactions in their lives so that they are free to give to the child without receiving much in return.

Many of the families who consider adopting a child do so for the humanitarian reason that they wish to help a child in need. It may very well be that they could help most by taking foster children instead, for there is an even greater need for good foster homes than for adoptive homes. This is particularly true for couples who already have some children of their own, for they are less 'child hungry' and can more easily share a child with his own family.

Social services departments and voluntary child-care societies are always glad to hear from people interested in fostering. If you write to let them know of your interest they will probably first send you some information and then invite you to a meeting or send someone to visit you at home and tell you more about their fostering services.

Before leaving the subject of fostering, we should briefly consider another section of the Children Act 1975 which has not yet been brought into force but which is potentially important to long-term foster parents and prospective adopters. It is a new kind of custody order called custodianship and will be half-way between adoption and fostering.

Like adoption, custodianship orders will be made by courts but, unlike adoption, they will not necessarily be permanent. Either natural parents or custodians will be able to go back to court and ask that the order be revoked.

Custodians will be able to make all the day-to-day decisions about the child's life, such as education and medical care. They will not be able to change the child's name or agree to adoption or emigration. When a custodianship order is made, a child previously in care of a local authority will go out of care, but the authority will be able to pay allowances to custodians probably along the lines of a fostering allowance.

The object of custodianship is to provide the child and the foster parents with greater security without the finality of adoption and without necessarily severing all ties with the child's original family.


HOLIDAY HOMES

People who can only have children in their homes for short periods, but enjoy child visitors, may like to offer a holiday home through the Children's Country Holiday Fund or some similar organisation. The object of these schemes is to give a few weeks of happy, healthy country living to children who would not otherwise have a holiday. This can also be a good way to provide an only child with some companionship during the summer holidays. Your local branch of the WRVS will probably be able to tell you more about it.

Most of these children come from underprivileged families and overcrowded homes; sometimes their mothers are strained and overtired or their fathers ill and unemployed. Many of them have never been away from home before. They may be confused by different standards and ways of eating or speaking and they will be quite unused to country life. Most of them will like fish and chips better than home-grown vegetables and they probably will not understand that if they chase the chickens there will be fewer eggs for breakfast. Looking after these youngsters is likely to keep you busy and both sides will have a lot to learn.

It is also possible to offer a permanent holiday home to a child who attends a special boarding school. These schools are for children who have emotional problems or mental or physical handicaps. Of course most of the children go to their own homes for the school holidays, but some children are 'in care' and cannot go home or can visit their parents only for a very limited period. These youngsters may urgently need a stable holiday foster home and providing this can be a deeply satisfying way of helping, particularly for couples who are not able to provide care to a child for fifty-two weeks in the year yet have a lot of love and interest to offer.

A number of local authorities and child care organisations run schemes whereby some of the children in their homes have a local 'uncle and auntie' who visit, take them on outings and sometimes have them for a holiday. The danger of this is, however, that the adults may lose interest after a while and then the child feels hurt and neglected.

Unless you can plan to keep up a regular contact and are prepared, if necessary, to go to considerable inconvenience in order to do so, it is best not to get attached to any particular child. Perhaps you can take a group of children on a picnic or for a day at the sea or the zoo. If you are clever at carpentry maybe you can make them a swing or a doll's house. Perhaps with a group of friends you can run a jumble sale or organise a concert to raise money for Christmas presents or some special piece of equipment. The main point is to be sure that you can carry through with any project you start on.

If you have a particular skill or interest there is sure to be some child who would like to share and learn. You might be able to help a talented little girl whose parents cannot afford music lessons or a boy who longs to learn fly-fishing but who has an invalid father. Maybe you could run an art class in a children's convalescent home, or have a backward but dependable boy to help in your garden. It may take time and trouble to find the youngster who wants and can benefit from your help, but it is well worth the effort.

FULL-TIME, PART-TIME AND VOLUNTEER JOBS

If you have time on your hands or a job which you feel is dull or unsatisfying you might like to consider full-time work with children or young people. In many areas there is a shortage of youth leaders, house-parents in children's homes, home helps etc. Most of these jobs require special training but it is often possible to get a grant which will cover the cost of this and give you a small living allowance. Maturity is a definite advantage for most of these professions and mature people are often accepted for training. All are challenging and worthwhile jobs which will give you endless opportunities to help children and will bring you great satisfaction.

A wide variety of part-time jobs may be available for people with suitable skills and experience and there is a constant, crying need for more volunteers. Help is needed with youth groups and clubs, scouts, guides, Sunday schools, young farmers' clubs, hospital visiting, parent-teachers' associations, and many other community projects.

Those who are prepared to give freely of their energy and interest, try out new ideas and methods and stick to a job even when they feel like giving up will be welcomed with open arms by hard-pressed organisation leaders. While you are helping others you will make new friends, get a new slant on some of the fundamental values in life and probably discover talents and abilities you did not know you possessed.

Being part of a church or community group whose members care for each other as well as helping others can also help to lessen the feelings of isolation and even worthlessness which many childless couples feel from time to time.

# CHAPTER VII

# Families of origin

(The chapter you must not skip)

It can be a great temptation to ignore the subject of your child's original parents or natural parents as they are sometimes called. Thinking about the two people who gave birth to the child that you have now made your own can be quite painful. If you are infertile, it is easy to feel jealous that someone else could give life; it is easy to feel angry at parents who have been cruel or neglectful; it is easy to fear the effect that knowledge of original parents might have on your beloved son or daughter or even that these people might actually reappear in your lives and cause difficulties.

All these feelings and fears are natural and many adoptive parents have them at some stage. But you are going to store up trouble and unhappiness for yourselves and your child unless you get over them and come to grips with the reality that this child, who is now a full member of your family, had his origins elsewhere, that these origins are important and that he has a right to know about them. The whole subject of explaining about adoption and helping your child to understand his own circumstances is discussed in later chapters. For the moment we must concentrate on facts and fantasies about the natural parents and your feelings about them.

Accepting the realities of your child's origins takes time and effort. It is rather like accepting infertility and both are an essential part of successful adoption. You will have to summon up all your sensitivity and imagination to put yourself in the shoes of a parent who has gone through the incredibly painful experience of bearing a child and parting with it or, even worse, having one's child removed forever by a court of law. Those of us who have led fairly sheltered, ordinary lives find it hard to understand how some people can get themselves into such miserable tangles. When you long for a child, it is difficult even to contemplate giving one up for adoption let alone just going off somewhere and leaving the child to its fate. Yet you must try to appreciate the problems that lie behind this behaviour. There is a very wise saying, to understand everything is to forgive everything. We can none of us reach the goal of total understanding, but we can aspire to it. Two adoptive parents who were well along this path, put their feelings this way when speaking of their children's first mothers. One said: 'I always feel close to Tim's mother because I know we both loved him.' And the other wrote in her account of an adoption: 'I could never forget Kathleen anyway. She gave me something which I could never have had without her and I take care for her of something she loved but could not keep.'


UNMARRIED MOTHERS AND FATHERS

A large proportion of the children placed for adoption are born out of wedlock whether they are joining their new families as infants or as older children. And in spite of the sexual freedom of our present era there is still much confusion, misunderstanding and difference of opinion about unmarried parents. Some people still think that the girls are mainly prostitutes. Others still believe these mothers are innocent girls raped by unscrupulous men or else look upon the fathering of an out-of-wedlock child as the wild oats normally sown by young men about town.

It is important that adopters know where the truth lies and also how they themselves feel about illegitimacy and the related questions of heredity. Both of these subjects touch deep-seated prejudices and attitudes in all of us. These may be unconscious and are likely to remain with us all our lives unless we take active steps to examine and perhaps change them. It is not enough to say 'Nobody thinks anything of illegitimacy nowadays.' You have to decide what you think about it and, more important, feel about it. Sometimes our true feelings are a little unexpected! The age old taunt of 'bastard' is still used and still hurts. If you have a niggling fear that an adopted child might be over-sexed or inherit a parent's promiscuous behaviour, you could be heading for trouble. Fears of this kind become self-fulfilling prophecies, so you need a solid background of facts about inheritance and about the social and emotional problems that may cause a parent to place a child for adoption.

Workers in social welfare agencies know that unmarried
mothers and those who are legally married but have their children out of wedlock, are of all types and all social groups. They
are shop assistants, secretaries, waitresses, nurses and factory
workers. A few are highly intelligent, a few are dull, most are
about average in ability and health.

Not many unmarried mothers are promiscuous, though plenty
of babies are born as a result of a casual encounter or short-lived
relationship. Prostitutes and those who sleep around usually take
careful precautions to make sure that they do not become pregnant. Very few mothers are the innocent victims of rape,
although many girls who seem highly sophisticated have, in fact,
been quite inadequately taught about either the physical or
emotional aspects of sex.

The traditional picture of unmarried mothers as over-sexed
women craving for sexual relationships is not upheld by the
evidence. It is, in fact, extremely rare for a person to be over-
sexed in the sense of having over-active sex glands, though this is
possible. The chances of an adopted child inheriting such a
condition are remote. Nor does the fact that she had an out-of-
wedlock child necessarily mean that the girl even enjoys sex.
Though many unmarried mothers are in love with the fathers of
their children, (or think they are) others are quite uninterested in
them and, far from being the sexy type, have very few boyfriends.

Many young people today accept sex before marriage as a
matter of course without always thinking through the possible
consequences. It is apt to be the most trusting and unsophisti-
cated who get caught. Many now have abortions but others feel
abortion is wrong, do not know where to go or leave it too late.
Others plan to keep the baby and, though many manage quite
well, others find that this proves to be too difficult.

While most single mothers are ordinary young women, a few
have severe personal problems such as serious emotional
immaturity, a mental illness or a history of inability to care for
their babies properly. Some are scarcely more than children
themselves.

Such a one was Lynette. She was still only 14 when her baby
was born, and her boyfriend was only a year older. Lynette had
spent her early childhood in Jamaica with her grandmother while
her mother came to England, got a job and had another child.
Lynette joined them when she was 10 but found the adjustment
to English life and schooling very difficult. She told the social
worker at the maternity hospital that getting pregnant was all a

big mistake. She did not feel ready to be a mother. She wanted to go back to school and train for a good job. Nor did she want to give her baby to her mother to bring up for they did not enjoy a close or loving relationship. Placing the child for adoption seemed the best plan for all of them.

Pauline at 37 was at the other end of the age scale. Well-educated and capable she was secretary to the manager of a big international company. They became lovers, he told her his marriage was unhappy and he was planning a divorce. Pauline had herself had an early, unsuccessful marriage. She longed to marry again and have a family. Her dreams were shattered when her boss suddenly returned to America and his wife. Pauline had known she was pregnant but had not told him. Now it was too late to get an abortion. Although Pauline had wished for a child, she wanted a family with a husband and security, not the struggle of a single parent trying to cope with a demanding full-time job and having her baby only in the late evening and at weekends. She wanted her child to have the sort of happy family life which she had not received herself (her parents had lived abroad and she had been sent home to relatives and boarding schools when she was 5). Pauline, too, felt that it was right to place her baby son for adoption and though it was a most painful decision she did not waver. It helped a great deal that the adoption agency arranged for her to meet the young couple who were to adopt and bring up her little boy. She liked them very much and felt confident that they would make good parents.

Samantha was a much more mixed-up person. She came from an outwardly respectable family and her brothers and sisters seemed well-adjusted and happy. But Samantha was always odd man out and was always at loggerheads with her parents. She went off to London when she was just 18, and got in with a group of young people squatting in derelict houses, drinking and using drugs. Her own health suffered badly and by the time she came to the attention of the staff in the maternity hospital they were deeply concerned about both her and the expected baby. She was a most attractive young woman and highly intelligent, but emotionally she was deeply disturbed. She found the routines of hospital unendurable, could not bring herself to make any sensible plans for her baby daughter and ended by discharging herself from the hospital and disappearing. The local social services department took the baby into care. They placed her with an experienced foster mother and after a rather difficult start, she began to thrive. When Samantha was still missing after six months, the department decided to place the baby with prospective adopters.

Mary's story is different again. Mary did not part with her little daughter Susan until the child was nearly 2 years old. She had considered adoption while she was pregnant but was persuaded by her friends in the office that it would be awful to give one's child away. She was lucky enough to be given a small council flat and she was sure she would manage even though her parents were so upset about the baby that they refused to help. As the months went on Mary found it harder and harder to be a single parent. Susan was a delicate baby and suffered from eczema which made her fretful. Neighbours complained about her crying. Mary had no friends on the council estate which was a long way from the town centre, the shops and her former friends. The bus service was poor and she had no money for taxis. The future looked bleak. Mary became very depressed. Sometimes she almost hated Susan when she would not stop crying and the eczema spoiled her appearance. On the advice of the health visitor, Mary approached a voluntary children's society for help. She had many discussions with the social worker who offered to try and get Susan a place in a day nursery and put Mary in touch with other young mothers with babies so she would not be so lonely. But in the end Mary decided that for Susan's sake and her own she should place the child for adoption. The realities of motherhood were not as pictured in the women's magazines. She felt she was missing all the fun her friends enjoyed and she worried about what sort of life she could give Susan. Adoption would give both of them another chance.

Unmarried fathers have tended to be rather shadowy figures but in some cases they need help and counselling just as much as the mothers. Paddy Boyle was shattered when his girl friend Sharon gave up their baby for adoption. These two young people came from the same little town in the south of Ireland and started living together when they met up in London and were lonely and homesick. When Sharon told him she was pregnant Paddy wanted to get married right away but Sharon was much more realistic. As a believing Catholic she saw marriage as a union for life and she did not think Paddy, with his fondness for going out with the boys and coming home drunk and who was sometimes violent, was going to be a reliable husband. She could not see how they were going to manage in two small furnished rooms with a landlord who did not like children and no place on the housing list. Their families back in Ireland would be shocked if they learned of the pregnancy but in any case they were in no position to help. To Paddy's great distress, Sharon broke off their relationship and later placed the baby with a Catholic adoption society. Paddy went to see the social worker. She explained that he could go to court and claim custody if he felt he could offer a good home for the baby but he could not otherwise prevent Sharon from placing the baby for adoption. Since Paddy could not offer a home at that time, there was nothing he could do.

Not all unmarried fathers are as concerned and interested as Paddy. Some try to deny paternity, others may be willing to contribute to the child's maintenance but do not want to be personally involved. Many, of course, have left the scene before the pregnancy is established and do not even know they are fathers. These days adoption agencies try hard to see the fathers of the babies they are placing both to get medical and social background information and to offer help to the young man in his own right. However, in a good many cases they do not succeed in making contact.

Background information may also be limited by the language and cultural barriers that occur in our multi-racial society. Social workers are not always able to provide a full and reliable picture of the child's personal and family history.

BROKEN FAMILIES

With separation and divorce rates running at an unprecedented level, it is inevitable that many children for adoption will come from broken homes even if they were not born illegitimate. Sometimes the parents' divorce is itself the reason for a child coming into care but more often it is the final stage of a series of family crises and one which makes the chance of re-establishing the home seem even more remote.

Marilyn married Jock when she was only 17. Her parents were very distressed because Jock had done badly at school and had already been in quite serious trouble with the police. However, he was a tall, good-looking boy and Marilyn was infatuated with him. She assured her parents she could manage him and there would be no more trouble. Alas this was not so. Marilyn had three pregnancies in rapid succession, including a set of twins. After a couple of years during which he worked steadily, Jock got into trouble again and was sent to prison for eighteen months. With four young children and very little money Marilyn's life became a nightmare. She did her best but was always in arrears with electricity bills or the rent. She was inevitably short-tempered with the children for she seldom had any relief from them, and they became increasingly out of hand and difficult to manage. When Jock came home things got worse rather than better. He started to gamble and their debts became worse. Finally they were threatened with eviction. Suddenly Marilyn cracked under the strain. She could stand it no longer. Leaving the children with a friend, she took off and went to a neighbouring city where she found a room and a job and started to think things out. Jock had never looked after the children and felt he could not cope so they were all admitted to care and placed in three separate foster homes as, except for one family taking the twins, there was nowhere for them to be together.

During the next two years Jock was back in prison, this time for a longer term. Marilyn felt terribly guilty about the children for she really cared about them, but she also felt a marvellous sense of freedom from a burden that would have taxed anybody's strength and which she had not in any way been ready to bear. After a while she met Hugh, a responsible hard-working young man. She wanted to divorce Jock, marry Hugh and start a new life. By this time three of the children had settled down well in their foster homes. The twins had been so young when they were placed that they could not remember living anywhere else. Their foster parents wanted very much to adopt them. The oldest girl Carol had formed a loving relationship with her foster parents and an older foster sister, so she, too, had a secure home. Only Mark, now aged 6, had been less fortunate. He and his first foster mother had just not got along and he was now in a small children's home though he still saw the twins and Carol sometimes. Marilyn visited all the children occasionally though she found the visits very painful and upsetting. The twins hardly knew her, Carol was much taken up with busy doings in her foster family and treated her mother in a rather off-hand way and Mark seemed confused by it all. Marilyn did not know what to say to him.

In a series of lengthy and often difficult discussions with the children's social worker and also with Hugh, Marilyn gradually came to the decision that it would be best for the twins and Carol to be adopted by their foster parents and for the social worker to find an adoptive family for Mark, hopefully one which would agree to occasional contact with his sisters. Marilyn just did not see how she could explain to any of the children if she took Mark home and let the others be adopted. She felt it would be wrong to uproot the twins from the only home they could remember, and in any case she was sure it would not work to expect Hugh to take on Jock's four children. She loved her children but they reminded her of a time in her life that she felt she must put behind her. Hugh would have been willing to take Mark but secretly hoped he would not have to do so. The boy looked exactly like his father and Hugh felt that their relationship would be difficult however hard he tried. The final goodbyes between Marilyn and the children were hard for all concerned, but the story has a cheerful ending – Mark was welcomed into a family with two girls who very much wanted a boy. He settled happily and did very well. Marilyn and Hugh established themselves in a comfortable home and eventually had two children.

## NEGLECTFUL PARENTS

Child neglect and abuse is something which makes most of us very angry and upset. Yet which of us could boast that we would never strike a crying child even when driven to the limits of our endurance? Which of us knows what we might do in the grip of a mental illness?

There are undoubtedly a few mentally unbalanced people who take a sadistic delight in inflicting mental or physical pain on a child, but such cases are very rare. Cruelty and neglect are usually perpetrated by damaged, deprived but basically well-meaning people who are at the end of their tether, or by those who are mentally handicapped or ill. It is one of the sad facts of life that some people who are not very bright or competent have to try and manage their lives in conditions that would test the ingenuity and endurance of the most intelligent and capable individual. Bad housing, a dreary deprived neighbourhood, lack of the domestic conveniences which most of us take for granted, and acute shortage of money create terrible problems for many families in our inner cities. It is not surprising that some of them sink under the strain and become known as 'problem families'.

When one looks into cases of child neglect there is almost always a long sad history, often going back for several generations. Rita's childhood was a confusing tangle of broken relationships. She was in and out of homes and foster homes and special schools in between being returned to her mother and step-father. At 16 she was on her own in lodgings but still barely able to read and write. She had a baby at 17 and reluctantly agreed that it should be placed for adoption. But when she became pregnant again she determined to keep the child. For a while she was able to live with the baby's father, an Indian whose wife and family had not yet joined him. When they did so of course Rita and little Darren had to move out. For a while they led a miserable life with bed and breakfast accommodation provided by the social services department in a run-down hotel. They had to walk round the town most of the day and eat their meals in cheap cafés. Then Rita met Len, a divorced man who worked as a labourer on building sites. He was staying in the same hotel. They managed to find some furnished rooms and Rita hoped she could settle down.

Unfortunately Darren, now nearly 2 years, was upset by all the moving around and became very difficult. He cried a lot and wet himself day and night. He was frightened of Len and always worse when he was around. Len thought Rita spoiled him and that he needed a firm hand. Len was not a cruel man but he was impatient and unimaginative and did not know his own strength. He often slapped Darren much too hard and neighbours complained to the NSPCC about the child's screaming. Rita was distressed but she was a bit afraid of Len herself and unable to stop him punishing Darren. One evening when he had had a couple of pints of beer and Darren was crying and grizzling, Len picked him up and flung him against the wall in a fit of temper. Darren lost consciousness and was rushed to hospital where he was found to have a broken arm and a cracked skull. There was a court case, Len was given a suspended prison sentence and both he and Rita were put on probation. After many anxious consultations, the social services department decided that it was too risky to allow Darren home again. Rita was too immature and needy herself to be an adequate mother. Her care of Darren was not very good at the best of times. Though she had broken off with Len for a while it seemed likely that she would go back to him for she could not really manage life on her own. It was decided that Darren should be placed in a foster home with a view to eventual adoption.

As these various stories show, the original parents of adopted children are of many different types and all social groups. Some of them have experienced special difficulties in growing up, in adjusting to adult life and in making lasting personal relationships. The decision to place their child for adoption is often the hardest they have ever had to make or will ever make again. Often it is the most thoughtful and responsible single mothers who decide on adoption as offering their child the best chance in life. It also takes maturity and unselfishness to agree to one's child being adopted by foster parents.

# CHAPTER VIII

# The adopted child's inheritance

If you take a packet of sunflower seeds and sow them in many different places they will not all grow the same way. Some will be straight and tall, others twisted and puny; some will be stunted and have few blossoms, others will bloom for weeks. It will depend on the soil and water supply, the sun and the weeds. But they will all be sunflowers. There will be fine and poor specimens of the sunflower family but no seed will turn into a rose-bush or a poppy.

When a human seed starts to grow certain characteristics are already settled. Among other things the unborn child's sex, the colouring and fingerprint pattern are determined and cannot be altered. Most other characteristics of appearance or personality are not so irrevocably fixed, but within this minute seed lie all the possibilities for the individual's future development. How these will in fact turn out depends on his environment, the family and nation he is born into, his illnesses, his friends and his enemies.

Out of a whole packet of sunflower seeds perhaps one or two seeds will be damaged or not properly formed even before they are planted. When they grow up into stunted or abnormal plants it may be difficult to tell whether the trouble was there from the start or whether the seed lacked the proper conditions for healthy growth. In the same way it is sometimes hard to say whether an unhealthy person was conceived with a defect or became ill because of his life experiences either before or after birth. Generally speaking, however, it seems that physical problems are rather more likely to be inherited than problems of personality. The latter are more often the result of upbringing.

We humans are extraordinarily complicated physically and

even more complicated mentally and emotionally. The more we learn about the wonders of human growth and development the more difficult the science of genetics (or heredity) seems to be. There is still much that we do not know but certain definite facts have been established and these are of vital interest and importance to anyone concerned with adoption.

In the first place we now feel sure that both heredity and environment are important. It is not a question of one or the other. We cannot afford to ignore hereditary factors, but at the same time no one can predict what sort of child will be born to a couple however much is known about them and their ancestors. There are so many thousands of possible combinations of characteristics that each baby might inherit and each of these characteristics will affect and be affected by his upbringing.

For instance, scientists have discovered that whether we are tall and thin or short and stocky largely depends on our heredity, but if a child is undernourished his growth will be stunted. Good food will not make him taller than his natural size but lack of food can make him smaller.

We inherit our colouring and basic features too, but a person's appearance depends also on his health, happiness and personality. Many of the most attractive men and women we meet do not have particularly good features but they have friendly, pleasant expressions, dress nicely and make the most of themselves. Anyone who has seen a neglected, unloved child blossom in a happy home will know how much appearances can change. Children actually come to look like the people who take care of them too. They adopt their parents' expressions, gestures and way of doing things. Strangers often remark on the resemblance between adopted children and their parents even though their features and colouring may be quite different.

We also know that children inherit from both their father and mother. However, they do not necessarily inherit the same appearance, ability or temperament as their parents because each parent carries a large number of hidden traits that either never develop or are masked by more powerful characteristics. These hidden traits can be passed on to the offspring. It accounts for the birth of a blue-eyed child to two brown-eyed parents or a person's striking resemblance to some ancestor. It also accounts for the birth of a very dull child to brilliant parents or a genius in an average family.

## SOME COMMON ERRORS

Much confusion about the dangers of heredity has been caused because people have thought that children inherited characteristics which their parents had acquired from their environment. Some adopters have blamed heredity for problems which were certainly due to faults in the upbringing which they themselves have provided. If a man loses a leg in a war we do not expect that his child will be born one-legged! But some people believe firmly that, if a man falls into bad ways and becomes a thief, his children will be thieves too.

This is not true. Some thieves are the children of thieves, but most are not. People steal for all sorts of reasons. Usually it is because they have deep psychological problems arising out of unfortunate life experiences, but sometimes it may be because they have not been properly taught that stealing is wrong. A child who lives among adults who steal is almost certain to steal also. Some thieves are handicapped by mental dullness or emotional instability, and it is possible that their children might inherit some of these characteristics. However, whether the children are honest or dishonest will depend upon the way they are brought up and their life experiences.

The same is true of skills and virtues. The child of a brilliant violinist may or may not inherit some musical ability. He certainly will not be born able to play the violin without training. The point is that we do not inherit specific skills, habits or kinds of behaviour. These we acquire as we grow up. We are born with certain characteristics which may develop for good or ill according to our upbringing. Stubbornness, for instance, can be an asset or a liability; extreme sensitiveness may be a handicap in certain situations but is an essential part of some of the most charming personalities; great physical energy may make a child boisterous and noisy but can help a man to the top of his profession. All through our lives our inborn tendencies and the external influences that surround us act and react on one another to produce our individual personalities.

Most of the characteristics which make people seem pleasant or unpleasant are the result of the way they are brought up and what they are taught. Kindness, honesty, loyalty and truthfulness are learned from parents and teachers and are attitudes of mind created by love and good experiences.

Every little child in the course of his development is unkind, tells tales and fibs and takes things which do not belong to him. In a happy family he gradually learns not to do these things, but at first they are quite normal and not signs of inherited cruelty or dishonesty. It is quite easy for most people to remember this when they are dealing with their own children because they do not expect them to be delinquent. It is not so easy for an adoptive parent who may be fearful about his child's background. This is why it is particularly important for adoptive parents to be as clear as possible about what is and is not inherited. Unless they understand they may not be able to be realistic about their child's behaviour or keep calm and continue to love and accept an adopted child as he grows through these normal though sometimes disturbing phases. Parents who always fear that their child will develop some undesirable characteristics may surround the youngster with so much tension that he actually develops the very symptoms they dread.

The father who spanks his 4-year-old son for telling stories because of his own fear that the boy will grow up to be a liar and a thief has forgotten or not bothered to find out, that this is normal behaviour for a 4-year-old child. The spanking is more likely to make the youngster a liar through fear of punishment than to lead him to an appreciation of the need for truth. One small girl announced to her startled mother that she had seen a lion in the garden. Her mother immediately sent her upstairs to say her prayers and tell God she was sorry for telling such lies. When she came down she said, 'I told God all about it and he said, "I quite agree with you, Miss Jones. I saw it there myself." '

## STUDIES OF ADOPTED CHILDREN

Various studies have been made of the way children with unsatisfactory family backgrounds have developed in adoption or foster homes. Some of the studies were done in America, some in France and Sweden and others here in Great Britain. Since human nature is the same all the world over the findings can be applied to similar situations in any country.

One of the very first such studies was done in 1922 in New York where the State Charities Aid Association studied 910 children who had been placed in families. All the children were over 18 at the time of the study and some were as much as 40 years old and had families of their own. Many of these 910 children had remained with their own parents for the first and most impressionable years of their lives and less than 10 per cent of them came from a background that was considered good.

Many of their parents were shiftless, immoral, alcoholic, in poor health, illiterate or dishonest, though of course others were normal citizens. In spite of their unpromising background, nearly 80 per cent of these children were found to be leading successful, honest lives and were considered capable individuals by those who knew them. They had not developed the weaknesses of their natural parents but had taken on the standards, attitudes and interests of those among whom they lived.

A much more recent study in Sweden showed that young men who had been adopted were no more likely to drink too much or have police records than other young men of the same age, even though a good many of their fathers were alcoholic or had a criminal record. A British research study in which 105 young adults and their adoptive parents discussed their experiences and feelings, found that nearly three-quarters of the young people were doing well in life and an even higher proportion of their parents felt that adopting had been a satisfactory experience. Of course there are some sad situations where adoptions have not worked out well, but ordinary families have their problems too and it would be unreasonable to suppose that every adoptive family will 'live happily ever after'. It is clear, however, that thanks to the happy, satisfying home life provided by their new families, adopted children seldom repeat the social problems of their original parents.

## WHY ADOPTERS MUST CONSIDER HEREDITY

This sort of information is most valuable and reassuring to adoptive parents but it does not mean that heredity does not count at all. Even the best environment can only develop what is already present in the individual. No amount of coaching can make a dull child clever or create artistic or musical ability, and it is important for ambitious adoptive parents to remember this. A realistic consideration of adoption involves such questions as how much parents will mind if their child does not want to stay in school any longer than absolutely necessary and shows more interest in cooking or motorcycle engines than in literature or arithmetic. If you are a rather academic family in which good school achievement is almost taken for granted, and if your interests lie in ideas, books and the arts rather than sport, craft or gardening, then you do need to consider seriously the strong possibility that an adopted son or daughter will not share these intellectual abilities and interests.

Though it is natural and right to hope to share interests and pleasures with one's children, it is ill-advised and unfair to adopt a child with the fixed idea of training him to some special skill or profession. One woman applied to adopt a child so that she could teach him French. Another couple hoped for a girl who would look after them in their old age. Some men want to adopt a son who will take over their business or keep up a family tradition. The chances are that the child's main interest will lie in some quite different direction from the parents' plans. Of course this can be equally true of born children, but people who have taken on children by deliberate choice are apt to feel rather differently about such things. Social workers with much experience in adoption often feel that planners who have every aspect of their family's life mapped out in advance are among the least suitable adopters.

Some of the saddest adoptions are those where the temperament or personality of the child and parents just do not suit one another. Sometimes the family seems to be quite successful on the surface but underneath both parents and child are baffled, frustrated and deeply disappointed by their inability to understand one another's point of view.

Most extreme situations of this sort can be avoided by wise and skilful placement of children in the homes best suited to their background and potentialities, although of course the younger the child, the more difficult this is to do and, as we have already seen, agencies are not always able to obtain full information about the child's background. Good adoption agencies no longer try to place all their children in the homes of highly educated people with great expectations. For many children they greatly prefer unpretentious families where parents will be delighted at any special abilities their child develops but will love him just as much without them. Children certainly need homes that will give them opportunities, but to live under the shadow of parental ambition or to find oneself a disappointment is a terrible burden for a young person to bear. It is almost bound to create a damaging sense of inferiority.

Glaring cases of really abnormal development in adopted children are rare, but every prospective adopter will do well to face the possibility that he may take on responsibility for a child whose temperament, likes and dislikes are very different from his own. Some people find this an additional challenge and enjoy the stimulation of differing personalities and points of view. Other families would find these adjustments too hard to make. Many of us are neither willing nor able to cope with children we find hard to understand; some people lack the patience, humour, insight and imagination that are needed; fortunately, others have enough and to spare. As Carol Prentice says in her book *The Adopted Child Looks at Adoption*,

> What the adopted parents themselves should pause to consider is their ability to meet the unexpected, to be tolerant of the uncongenial and alien personality, to respect a child's individuality and help him develop his proper self without regard to the personal preferences of his adopted family.

### ARE SOME PHYSICAL ILLNESSES INHERITED?

Some illnesses can be inherited although most of them are not, so it is always wise to inquire about the family health history of a child being considered for adoption. A full health history on both parents and their families is helpful and will be important if there is inheritable illness in the child's family. If necessary, you may want advice from a doctor or a specialist in heredity. You will no doubt be willing to take reasonable risks even if you are hoping for a healthy baby; after all, a child born to you might inherit or develop some illness or defect. But this is different from adopting a sick child knowingly. If you are offering a home to a physically handicapped child, you will want full information about the child's present condition, his own health history and his family health history so that you can take on problems with your eyes open.

Some diseases and malformations such as dwarfism or extra fingers are known to be hereditary but most of these are very rare and need not concern the average adopter. Epilepsy is an illness which is slightly more common and one which people are inclined to be especially worried about. Doctors think that there is an hereditary factor involved in many cases of epilepsy though others are caused by birth injuries or later accidents. People who are epileptic as a result of injuries would not pass the problem to their children. Even when there is a hereditary factor, environment may well determine whether the illness actually manifests itself.

There are several important points to remember in connection with epilepsy. One is that modern drugs can often prevent and almost always control epileptic seizures. Another is that for every 100 children with an epileptic parent only three to six will themselves develop epilepsy. The rest will be quite free from the disease. Many perfectly normal babies have convulsions when they are teething or have a high temperature and, though they should of course receive expert medical attention, it does not usually mean that these children will be epileptic.

Allergies causing eczema, hay fever and asthma are quite often inherited though stress in the environment can make them much worse. There is also an hereditary element in many cases of diabetes, deafness and heart disease. Medical opinion is divided about whether there is some hereditary susceptibility to some other illnesses such as ulcers, rheumatic fever and certain kinds of tumours. Children coming from families with a history of these diseases may be somewhat more likely to develop them than the average member of the population. None of these illnesses is inherited directly, however, and the risks are slight.

If you are considering adopting a child with a poor family health history it is helpful to have the advice of a doctor with a particular interest in problems of inheritance. At the same time you might keep a sense of proportion by reviewing your own family health history. In all probability some of your relatives, aunts, cousins, grandparents or even your own father and mother have suffered from quite severe illnesses from time to time. Some of these could possibly have been inherited by you or your children, but this probably would not deter you from having a child of your own if you could.

All good adoption agencies will have had the child medically examined before introducing him to you. They will usually arrange for you to talk to the agency medical adviser if there are medical problems. Though no doctors can guarantee you a healthy child they can usually detect severe abnormalities even in very young babies. The agency also will be able to tell you the relevant facts that are known about the child and his family. Case histories are, however, somewhat apt to contain more information about difficulties than successes. If you hear about some of the child's ancestors who were ill or social misfits it is helpful to remember that the other relatives you have not heard about were probably honest, healthy, unexciting citizens.

IS IT UNWISE TO ADOPT A CHILD WHO HAS A PARENT IN A MENTAL HOSPITAL?

Many people are still confused about the difference between

mental handicap and mental illness. A mentally handicapped person is someone whose intelligence has not developed properly. Some never learn to speak or look after themselves but many are just very dull mentally. Some live in hospitals or institutions because their families cannot care for them but most can get along in the community with special help and support. People can be born handicapped or become so through illness or accident, but, unfortunately, we do not have the means to cure real mental handicap. A mentally handicapped child can be helped to make the very most of his abilities but he cannot be 'cured' and become normal.

Mentally ill people are those whose intelligence developed normally but they became ill later in life. Their illnesses range from mild nervous breakdowns or depressions to those distressing cases of people who no longer know who or where they are and are quite incapable of living in the community. We are beginning to understand that mental illnesses are of many different kinds, some much more serious than others. A great many can now be cured. Every year, thousands of people go into psychiatric hospitals, get treatment and return home to their normal lives. Nevertheless many people are still more afraid of mental illness than of physical illness and we still have a great deal to learn about it.

Studies of the relatives of people in mental hospitals seem to show that with a few exceptions mental illnesses are not actually inherited, but the members of some families seem to be more prone to become ill in this way than others. It appears that some of us are born more able than others to withstand the shocks and trials of life. This emotional toughness or tenderness seems to be largely inherited but, of course, it is the environment that determines how much we are put to the test.

This is well illustrated by the story of twin sisters whom we will call Jill and Joan. They were the children of a mentally ill mother and an alcoholic father. Joan was sent to live with some relatives when she was about 2 years old and she had a good, wholesome upbringing. Her sister Jill remained with her sick parents and very soon she too showed signs of mental instability. She was in and out of a mental hospital all her life and was a most disturbing influence on all who knew her. Joan seemed to be a perfectly normal woman and had no special problems until she was about 50 years old. Then she again came in contact with her twin. There was a great deal of trouble and unpleasantness over their father's will and during this same period Joan had other serious difficulties to contend with. Soon she was overcome by these strains and became ill herself.

One can see in this story how both these children inherited a tendency to become ill under unusual stress. Jill, who remained in an unhealthy environment, was affected by it when she was still very young. Joan might have lived all her life without succumbing to mental illness if she had not had to cope with a number of unpleasant problems all at once.

A number of children placed for adoption have a parent with a history of mental illness. Indeed the illness may be the reason the child needs an adoptive family. If such a child is suggested to you, you will want to get expert advice about what it all means. Your own doctor or the agency medical adviser will very likely be able to help. They may also suggest that you obtain a specialist's opinion on the risks for the child.

## HOW ABOUT THE INTELLIGENCE OF ADOPTED CHILDREN?

In recent years a great deal has been discovered about the relative influence of environment and heredity upon intelligence. We now believe that a child's basic intellectual ability is inherited, but whether that ability is ever fully used depends almost entirely on the environment. Most people do not use all the brains they were born with. Apparent intelligence is the result of education, social training and opportunities almost as much as actual brain power. People who are fortunate enough to come from homes which provide many opportunities for learning and for developing wide interests, sometimes appear to be more intelligent than they really are. Conversely, people from very limited environments may seem rather dull when they are really quite clever.

Nevertheless a child's intelligence is not very likely to be startlingly different from that of his parents. We cannot predict a child's intelligence accurately but we do know that in this area heredity is rather important.

Most adopted children come from families that are about average in basic intelligence but have often been unable to develop their potentialities because of poor environment or emotional problems. The chances are therefore that adopted children will seem somewhat more intelligent than their natural parents because they are likely to have much better opportunities.

Every year a certain number of mentally handicapped people

have children out of wedlock and some of these become available for adoption. You may well ask, if intelligence is largely hereditary, how can these children possibly be considered suitable?

The answer is that here again one cannot safely generalise. Each child is an individual and must be considered separately. We have to remember that children inherit from their fathers as well as their mothers. Much also depends on the family history. If the mother was normal at birth and became mentally handicapped because of illness or injury, her child will not be affected. The situation here is the same as that of the man who loses a leg in an accident but has a two-legged son. However, if the mother's parents or brothers and sisters are also mentally dull or there is a long history of family backwardness or instability the outlook is less promising and the child may be backward too. One fairly reliable estimate by a specialist in problems of inheritance is that one-quarter of the children of the mentally handicapped will themselves be mentally backward but the rest will be about average. However, a study of 150 children born to seventy-three mentally retarded mothers showed that 90 per cent of the children came within the normal range of intelligence. Some of these were dull, some average and a few superior. Only 10 per cent of the children were truly mentally handicapped.

Some forms of mental handicap can be detected by doctors at birth or very soon after. A child who has been properly medically examined before placement is very unlikely to turn out grossly abnormal unless he later suffers from some unexpected illness. It is not possible, however, to detect the less obvious forms of backwardness for several months at least. If a baby has been born premature and delicate, or if it was a very difficult birth with a possibility of injury, it may be at least a year and perhaps longer before the child's future capacity can be reliably estimated.

There are standard tests which psychologists can give to older children and which give a reasonably accurate picture of the youngster's intellectual ability. However, if a child has had a bad start with poor care or many changes of home and school he may test lower than his real capacity. Many children's school work improves enormously once they get settled into a good family with plenty of encouragement and support. However, it is no good adopting a child whose mental ability is definitely slow and expecting that you can turn him into a good scholar. You can only help him to make the very best of his abilities, and these may remain quite limited. A Down's Syndrome baby, for instance, will not 'grow out of it' and become like other children.

## PROBABILITIES AND CHANCES OF INHERITANCE

No intelligent parents expect to bring up perfect children nor do they even hope to have family life without problems. They know that the successful family is the one that has learned to solve its difficulties together.

The question in the adopter's mind therefore is how much greater are the risks and difficulties we face in having an adopted rather than a 'born' family? Let us consider first some of the obvious advantages adoptive parents have over natural parents.

In the first place they have children by deliberate choice. In many households children just come along. They are loved on arrival but were not planned or even specially wanted. Then, too, adopters can have some choice about the sex and age of their child, a privilege not given to natural parents.

It is most unlikely that adoptive parents will unknowingly become responsible for a severely defective child nor one that is deformed or blind. People having their own babies take these risks and out of every 100 babies born, one or two will have some sort of abnormality.

On the other side of the coin you will probably know less about the family history of your adopted child than you would about your own. But how much less? Many people know very little about their more distant relatives, so quite often a child will have only a few more unknown ancestors than do his adoptive parents.

An adopted child might possibly inherit some less desirable characteristics that you could not have passed on to him, but he is just as likely to have some inherited talent or pleasing trait which you could not have given him. It works both ways. The chances are, however, that an adopted child may be less like you in personality or intelligence than your born child would be. Do you mind about a child fitting closely into your traditional family pattern? Will it worry you if he decides to take up some unusual form of employment or marries outside your social circle? The average adopted child is likely to be just that. Average. Not perhaps average for your family or social group but average for society as a whole.

These can only be very broad generalisations, and each couple faces special circumstances composed of their own life situation, hopes and anxieties and the particular information, or lack of it, that is available about the child. They must decide for themselves how much risk they feel able to take. Some people can be comfortable with greater risks and uncertainties than others.

Most people have some doubts and fears and feel that they could cope with some problems but not with others. A good adoption agency will respect such feelings and be glad to discuss any difficulties you may have.

The important thing is not to undertake responsibility for a child whose history, family background, appearance or intelligence you feel really anxious about. Your fears may be groundless or well-founded. This does not matter. What does matter is that over-anxiety in parents can actually create problems in a child. We all know mothers who always think their children are delicate or ill and run after them trying to protect them against wet feet, rough play and so on. In some cases, though the children are basically quite healthy, they develop constant coughs and colds or aches and pains just from the power of suggestion. This is fairly obvious.

What is less easy to see, but often no less true, is that parents who are too eager for their child to show signs of high intelligence may actually make the child so tense that he cannot learn; parents who expect deceitful behaviour are apt unconsciously to encourage such behaviour; parents who are too afraid that their teenager's normal interest in the opposite sex will become excessive and out of hand are likely to have rebellious or repressed youngsters to deal with.

Adoptive parents do need some extra wisdom. They need to be adaptable and perhaps above all they need a sense of humour that will give them a sense of proportion and carry them over the rough patches. They also need a sturdy belief in the over-riding importance of upbringing in determining how their child will develop.

# CHAPTER IX

# Early experiences

## THE IMPORTANCE OF ENVIRONMENT

When a child goes to a new home he does not start fresh with a clean slate. He takes his past with him. Only too often this past is full of uncomfortable, frightening experiences. It seldom happens that a youngster spends his first few years with loving, capable parents and is then placed for adoption. He is much more likely to have endured a series of moves and partings, some good care, some poor care, but, above all, much uncertainty and change. A little child that is moved from foster home to foster home by an irresponsible or desperate mother suffers terribly from fear and confusion. A child brought up in a hospital or children's home suffers from lack of individual love and attention. In either case he may not have been able to develop properly either mentally or emotionally and he may bear the scars of these experiences for many years – perhaps for ever. They will show in his behaviour, his distrust of adults and his overriding fear that he will lose his mother and father too.

Adoptive parents usually, and rightly, expect to find out something about the inheritance of any child they hope to make part of their family. It is rather more important to enquire about life experience. Even quite young babies will have a life history which you need to know. Did the mother have ante-natal care? Were there any complications in the delivery? What was the baby's condition at birth? Have there been any feeding problems? If he has been in a temporary foster home, what sort of household has he been used to? What are his normal routines?

If you are taking into your home a child of more than a few weeks old there will be many more questions to ask. Some of the most important are: how many changes of home has the child experienced? Where did he live and who looked after him? What sort of people were they? Are any of them still important to him? When did he last see his parents and under what circumstances? Has he spent any periods in hospital? If so, how long? How many schools has he been to and what were they like? Only when you know the answers to these questions will you have any idea of the experiences your child has already had to contend with, what you may expect from him and the sort of help he may require.

People who adopt older children also need a firm grasp of the normal patterns of human development. All older children moving into new families have suffered disruptions and deprivations of various kinds. They also show behaviour disorders of one sort or another. If you know something about child development and can work out at what stages your child suffered loss, change or inadequate care, then you will be better able to understand why he behaves the way he does and what to do to help him get over it.

There is a normal sequence of physical, mental and emotional development which all children need to grow through. We learn to crawl before we walk, to babble before we talk and to scribble before we write. If the usual sequence of growth is interrupted or distorted, it can cause a lot of trouble later. This is particularly likely to happen with emotional development. The child may have to go back and catch up on some of the stages he missed or which became muddled. It is therefore helpful if adoptive parents of older children are familiar with the development and behaviour patterns of younger children too. Reference to the child's life experience may reveal that he is reacting to some event in the past which caused his development to get stuck. This does not mean that he should be allowed to continue the misbehaviour, but it may provide clues as to how best to deal with the problem.

The effects of some life experiences are obvious and easily understood. Others are much more subtle and could well be overlooked. Imagining the feelings of a child who has been openly abused or rejected is not difficult. It is much harder to appreciate what it would be like to be cared for by a succession of nurses, foster parents or residential staff all with their own ideas and ways of doing things. Yet the effect of this can be equally damaging. It is easy to understand that a child who has witnessed violent quarrels between his parents will probably be frightened and upset by arguments in a new family. It may be more difficult to realise that failure to learn to read could be due to incessant worry about what has happened at home or what will happen in the future. Leslie was 11 years old but he could not read at all. As part of the preparation for moving into a new family, his adoption worker began to help him make sense of what had happened in the past. She discovered that he did not even know his mother's name and did not understand that she had died. His last recollection was of her being taken away in an ambulance. He was then 5 years old. After he had been on a visit to her grave, he learned to read and write almost at once and when his teacher asked why he could not do it earlier he replied quite simply, 'I had nothing to read and write about before.'

## THE EARLY YEARS

One of the interesting and unexpected findings of research on child development is that what makes a bad environment for a baby or young child is not what we generally consider a bad environment at all. The very worst place for a child to live is somewhere he is not loved. It does not matter too much if a child's home is a bit dirty and scruffy as long as he himself is loved and wanted. Such a home is always preferable to a scientifically run hospital or institution where he may have wonderful physical care, a clean bed to himself, fresh air, well-balanced meals, but, and it is a big but, not enough love, no petting and cuddling, no warm, physical contact with a mother person. The most dramatic cases are those of the babies that literally pine away and die under these circumstances. Others do not show their hurt so openly but are none the less severely damaged. A few seem to survive such experiences unharmed. In contrast to this, many so-called neglectful homes have produced children that are happy, healthy and do well in life.

There is now quite conclusive evidence that babies need loving just as much as feeding. Above all, they need a mother person to attach themselves to if they are to thrive. It need not be the woman who gave birth to the child, and fathers can 'mother' too in this sense. Though most nurseries and hospitals now try to give the children as much affection and individual attention as possible, no institution, however well run, can ever take the place of a family. Most normal babies and young children are now placed in foster homes rather than residential nurseries, but there are still thousands of physically and mentally handicapped children being brought up in hospitals.

As a good mother reliably satisfies her baby's need, he comes to love and trust her and then to wish to please her. This is the basis on which we have all learned to make personal relationships, to give as well as take and to be aware of the feelings and needs of other people. From this beginning comes the development of conscience and a wish and ability to control behaviour and impulses so as to be loved and accepted. Learning to do this takes time.

Even in ordinary families without the changes and upsets which occur in adoption, much of the adult world is very confusing to a young child. The normal 3-year-old's everlasting questions are part of his effort to understand cause and effect. When there has been no order in a child's life he cannot begin to make sense of it and, since many unpleasant things appear to have happened as punishment for his naughtiness, the little child tends to assume that all painful events are the result of his badness. The acute pain of separation from parents or well-loved foster parents must, surely, be due to very great badness. According to circumstances and temperament, some children will take this inwardly with withdrawn behaviour and nervous symptoms, while others react with anger and aggression. Both sorts of behaviour are the child's way of warding off painful feelings of anxiety and guilt. They can only be given up as the child is helped to understand what is happening and why. It is a major task for new parents to help their child come to terms with what went on in the past and we shall need to come back to this in later chapters.

LOVING AND LOSING

Sheep and their lambs can recognise each other within a few minutes of birth; ducklings follow the mother duck or the motherly hen which brooded them. All young creatures that are dependent on the care of the parents, attach themselves to them in their need for protection, food and warmth. Babies do the same.

In the human species, the bond of affection between child and parents is of vital importance not only as a means of securing care and attention in infancy but also because it sets the pattern for the child's ability to relate to others. It is the foundation stone of personality. The bond does not have to have a physical basis. On the parents' side it grows from caring for the child, not from giving birth. On the child's side it is partly instinctive, partly a response to loving care provided by the mother person.

Until about the age of 6 months, babies attach themselves fairly easily to whoever is looking after them and usually accept a change of caretaker without too much difficulty. There are, of course, individual variations. Some infants are particularly sensitive and even at a very young age they may be deeply distressed by a change of home.

From 6 months onward, virtually all babies become shy with strangers and most toddlers will only play happily within easy reach of their mothers. Surprisingly, it is the children who are most secure in their relationship with their parents who can best tolerate separation from them and most quickly attach themselves to someone else. If the parent has not been able to provide warm, continuous and reliable care, the child is likely to react strongly to being parted. He cannot cope with separation because he cannot be sure that his parents will come back; he cannot predict their behaviour so he is anxiously clinging and does not readily trust anyone.

Loss of a parent is bound to be a major emotional upset even to the most secure child. The normal pattern of reaction is that the child first protests, then mourns and is depressed and then gradually recovers. If he has had previous good relationships, he will have a capacity to make new ones; the wound heals and he is able to resume normal emotional development with only a little scar. If former relationships were not secure, or if they have been broken too often, there is a real danger that the youngster's capacity to attach will have been damaged. The risk is that his reaction to further change will be the kind of unattractive behaviour which causes rejection and yet more loss and change, and so a vicious circle is set up which if not successfully interrupted can only lead to serious trouble.

It is advisable for adoptive parents to find out as much as possible about their child's past relationships though this information may be difficult to obtain. Do not assume that because a parent was less than adequate, the child will not be attached and will not need to mourn. Children often love deeply quite neglectful or even cruel parents. You cannot undo the pain of past losses, but, if you understand what has happened, it will be easier to allow your new child to grieve and not expect him to transfer his love and loyalty too quickly. Mourning is a sign of health. When a loss occurs, grief is normal and necessary. The danger sign is when a child is superficial and moves too easily because he has never learned how to form deep attachments or has given up trying. If your child has this problem, he is likely to need professional help as well as lots of love and care from you.

## BEING 'IN CARE'

Being 'in care' is a shorthand for saying in care of a local authority or a child care agency. It sounds secure and comfortable but unfortunately that is by no means always the case. It is very difficult for any public body to take the place of parents. The main problems are changes of staff (which mean that lasting relationships are impossible), the difficulty of making allowances for individual needs while treating all the children fairly, and the sense of stigma which seems to be felt by all children who are in public care. Children ask each other prying and sometimes cruel questions and it seems almost impossible to prevent children at school from being known as the 'home children' and feeling set apart and inferior. Even those living in foster homes may have difficulty explaining their status to their friends.

In most children's homes as well as in hospitals and boarding schools, staff work a shift system, which means that they can have reasonable time off and may even live in their own homes. It also means that the children have to adjust to a succession of caretakers with differing expectations and attitudes. The children are kindly treated, but too often no one is deeply interested in their achievements or worries. No one is urging that little bit of extra effort at school or sports or encouraging them to persist with a hobby or interest in face of difficulties. It is all too easy for children in residential care to learn to 'play the system' and manipulate staff who cannot know exactly what has been agreed by someone on the previous shift. When Jerry lost a tooth he managed to get 10p from three different members of staff none of whom knew the others had given to him.

A child who has spent a considerable period in group care will lack basic information about family life. If he has lived in a hospital or large institution, he may never have seen food cooked or prepared and may never have been to a grocery or a butcher's shop. Even in smaller children's homes, toys, clothes, and household supplies appear as though by magic. The children often have very little idea of the value of things and may be terribly careless and extravagant. A children's home is in some ways too much a children's world. They hear little adult conversation and are not used to the emotional demands of family life, to adults showing affection to each other or getting angry with each other, or even to adults always being there. 'When do you go off duty?' is a quite usual question from a child who has newly joined a foster or adoptive family. It may sound amusing, but it discloses in a rather pitiful way the depth of that youngster's ignorance about normal family life.

CAN A BAD START BE OVERCOME?

Just as physical development can be stunted by very inadequate food, so emotional development can be stunted or warped by the disruption of relationships or by lack of opportunities to form the strong bonds of affection which nourish a child's emotions. The extent of the damage will depend not only on the severity of the deprivation and how long it lasted, but also on the child's own emotional strength. Some children are constitutionally more robust than others.

Fortunately children are marvellously resilient beings. Some, like Emma, are born survivors. Emma was born with quite severe facial disfigurement and was immediately rejected by her parents. In spite of a failed foster home placement, two years in a residential nursery, several operations and innumerable visits to hospital clinics, Emma maintained her cheerful, matter of fact approach to life along with an amazing optimism. At the age of 4 years she could explain to the clinic doctor: 'My first family didn't want me because of the way I looked.' Later that same day she waved goodbye to her visiting social worker with the usual reminder: 'Don't forget to get me a new mummy and daddy.'

Given time and the right sort of help, most children recover from a bad start even if they still bear some scars. Some, however, may suffer rather long-lasting emotional handicaps and need psychological or psychiatric help to overcome them. It is well for adoptive parents of older children to bear this in mind and be prepared to seek professional advice and counselling when necessary. Their child's need for this extra help is not likely to be a reflection on their own care of him but will almost certainly be due to long-lasting damage inflicted years before. The adoption agency will either provide the help themselves or suggest where it can be obtained.

If you are asked to consider a child whose life history is full of pain and partings, it will be wise to ask if he has been psychiatrically assessed. A child psychiatrist will usually be able to judge how much emotional damage the child has suffered, give some indication of the chances of full recovery and make some suggestions of the kind of care, treatment and management likely to help most. If the agency has not already had this assessment done, you may want to suggest it. The child's future is at stake and nothing should be too much trouble.

Both large scale research studies and the individual experiences of adoptive families show that though there are some disappointments and disruptions, the adoption of older and emotionally damaged children often works minor miracles and occasionally major ones.

A baby who has been deprived of mothering may have to learn to love. An older child, who is not used to being kissed or made much of, may seem lacking in response and affection for his new parents. He may be affectionate to one parent but not the other. This is hard for new parents to take. They feel they have so much love to offer and it is apparently turned down. As one disappointed adoptive mother said about her child, 'She didn't help you to love her.' What this mother had not realised was that it was up to her to help this child learn to be affectionate. She needed to give unselfishly and without limit before she could expect the child to love her in return. She needed to teach her child how to love.

There is not a person in the world who does not need loving, however much he or she may pretend not to. There is not a baby born who does not have a capacity to give and receive love. This capacity may be stunted and hidden but it is seldom extinguished altogether. We all long to be loved and wanted and important to somebody. It takes maturity and an ability to give generously of oneself, to go on loving a child or person who does not seem to love back. But this is what many adoptive parents are called upon to do at first. When their new child seems cold or unresponsive, if they too pull away in hurt disappointment or anger, then the child's chance is gone. If they can go on steadily offering love, acceptance and support, not forcing their attentions on the child but just making him aware of their love and longing to make him part of their family just as he is, then the crusts of fear and distrust will gradually crumble away and in his own time and his own way he will be able to respond. It may take a year or occasionally even more. Love and friendship won in this way are often much more worthwhile than the shallower kinds which are given at once, but it may be hard waiting and you may need help and support from your social worker and from other adoptive or foster parents.

# CHAPTER X

# Some legal requirements

In a book like this, it is not possible or appropriate to give detailed legal information. Also, adoption law is in the process of change while the Children Act 1975 is being gradually brought into force. This chapter is only intended to be a general guide to the legal framework and you will need to seek more precise and detailed information from the adoption agency, the court or your solicitor.

Since adoption is a legal process it is regulated by law and can only be completed in the courts. In England and Wales adoption orders can be made by the High Court, a county court or a magistrates court. In Scotland adoptions are dealt with in the Sheriff's Court and the procedure is slightly different. Only as a result of an adoption order can the child become a full member of your family. Once the order is made the child takes your name and belongs with you permanently. By law the child is now yours as though he had been born to you and he has no legal ties to any other family. The court has a right to impose terms and conditions for the granting of an order but very rarely does so.

Most applications are made to the county or magistrates courts where the proceedings are simple and the cost normally very small. The case is heard in private with only the judge or magistrates and a few officials present and is usually a very informal, brief affair. The necessary investigations are completed beforehand. Only if the adoption is contested by the natural parents do the legal proceedings become complicated and potentially expensive. If it is a straightforward case you will not need a lawyer in England or Wales but you will need one in all cases in Scotland.

When you take a child through an adoption society or social services department, you will be given advice about the necessary legal procedures. If you plan to take a child from some other source, you would probably be wise to make inquiries in advance at your local court or social services department. The officials there will tell you how to notify the necessary authorities and how and when to apply to the court for an adoption order. It will be particularly important to make these inquiries if you wish to take a child abroad with you because then the legal situation may be more complicated.

CONSENTS (now called agreements)

Before an adoption order can be made the court must be satisfied that all the people concerned understand what they are doing. Agreement to the adoption must be obtained from the child's parents or guardians, and if the child is old enough to understand what is happening, his agreement is needed too. The agreement of a married mother's husband may be required even if the child is not his.

The adopters and the child have to appear in court for the hearing, but it is seldom necessary for the natural parents to do so, unless they wish to contest the adoption. They can sign their agreement in advance and have it witnessed by a JP or court officer.

It is also possible for parents to give their agreement without knowing the name of the adopters, who can be referred to by a serial number. This is a great advantage. Unless the mother already knows you, you should ask for a serial number when applying to the court for the necessary papers.

The rights of natural parents have to be carefully guarded. It is not enough to say that the adopters could give the child a better home and more advantages. Parents have a right to their children unless they have very obviously failed even to try to provide for them. If the parents are mentally incapable, cannot be found or have persistently failed without reasonable cause to discharge their parental duties, the court may dispense with their agreement. Abandonment, neglect and either persistent or serious ill-treatment can sometimes be considered grounds for dispensing with agreement or ruling that agreement is unreasonably withheld, though leaving a child unvisited in an institution or foster home is not legally abandonment.

In the past the courts were greatly concerned to protect the rights of natural parents and did not consider the welfare of the child to be their first responsibility. This attitude has changed very considerably in recent years. The child's right to a secure and happy home is increasingly accepted. The Children Act 1975 laid down that when making any decision relating to the adoption of a child, agencies and courts must 'give first consideration to the need to safeguard and promote his welfare throughout his childhood.'

Until quite recently a parent could leave a child in care indefinitely with no plan to take him home later and yet prevent him being placed for adoption. Now that courts are more sympathetic to the needs of the child, agencies are much more likely to go ahead and plan an adoption placement even though it is probable that there will be a legal dispute when the time comes to apply for an adoption order. You may be asked by the agency if you are willing to take a child with the risk of a contested hearing. This is something to think about carefully. The agency will, no doubt, have sought legal advice and be reasonably confident about winning the case, but legal battles are anxious, painful proceedings and can be very expensive. You should certainly find out if the agency is able and willing to reimburse you for any major legal costs which you may incur in such cases and be quite clear about where you stand on this point.

Since 1976, foster parents who have cared for a child for five years or more have a definite right to an adoption hearing if they want one. Once these foster parents have notified their local authority of their intention to apply for an adoption order, neither the authority nor the natural parents may remove the child before the court hearing. (A formal application to adopt must be made to the court within three months or this 'freezing' provision will lapse.) Of course foster parents cannot be sure that the court will grant the adoption order, but at least they can now be sure of getting a hearing.

In a traditional baby adoption, the mother cannot sign a legal agreement to adoption until her child is 6 weeks old, for it is felt that she will not be in a fit state to make a decision immediately after her confinement. But, even when she has agreed, her rights continue until the adoption order is actually signed by the judge or magistrate. This means that until that moment the mother is able to change her mind and ask to have her child back.

Inevitably this is a source of great anxiety to the adopters, who live in dread of losing the child they are growing to love. In actual fact very few mothers claim their children back after placing them, especially if adequate social services are available and they have had an opportunity to come to a thoughtful decision. If the mother has changed her mind several times, or allowed a long period of time to elapse before trying to reclaim the child, or if she has no adequate plan to care for him herself, the court may consider that she is being 'unreasonable' and grant the order anyway. Nevertheless, these uncertainties are a source of real difficulty for the new adoptive family trying to settle down together, and the present need to keep re-affirming their agreement is a source of pain and distress to many mothers. A section of the Children Act 1975, which has not yet been brought into force, will make it possible to have a child 'freed for adoption' by the court at a much earlier stage in the proceedings. This will remove the burden of anxiety for all concerned and be a much more satisfactory arrangement.

### NOTIFICATIONS TO WELFARE AUTHORITIES

The present arrangement is that before you can set the legal processes in motion, you must send a formal notification to the social services department of the local authority in which you live, telling them that you have a child in your care whom you wish to adopt. It is the duty of the local authority to supervise and 'secure the well-being' of children who have been placed for adoption unless such children are already in the care of a local authority.

Prospective adopters must have the child in their care for at least three months before an adoption order can be made and the child must be 6 weeks old before this 'probationary period' can begin. This may seem a hard rule but it is a wise one. It takes time to grow into a family, and until parents and child have lived together for a while neither they, nor anyone else, can be sure that adoption is going to be in the best interests of all concerned. There is no need to apply for adoption papers immediately and, especially if the child is beyond infancy, it quite often takes much more than three months for the new family to settle down together. This is the time for learning to live together. Once the order is made it will be too late for either adopters or natural parents to change their minds. Although unnecessary delay should be avoided, at no point is adoption something which should be rushed.

When your application for an adoption order is received by the court, a guardian *ad litem* will be appointed to investigate the circumstances of the adoption, interview all the people concerned, including the natural parents, and make a full report to the court. The guardian *ad litem* will probably be one of the staff of the social services department or a probation officer. He or she may, or may not, be the same person who has been visiting you from the welfare authority.

## MAKING USE OF SOCIAL WORKERS

As you can see, you may be visited by quite a number of social workers before your child is finally adopted, the health visitor, your own agency worker, the welfare supervisor and the guardian *ad litem*. This may have its tiresome moments but can be a help too.

Right at the beginning try to rid yourself of two popular misconceptions. First, that social workers are trying to prove that you are incapable parents or are hoping to take your child away. Second, that social workers are either domineering, elderly busybodies or incompetent, young radicals.

In reality, the social workers who visit you are likely to be firm believers in the value of good adoptions and keen to help you make yours a success. You will probably both like and respect them. If you are unlucky and find that one of them is uncongenial or seems to lack experience in adoption work, you will just have to do your best to work with her (or him) for the sake of the child.

'Your' social workers may be almost any age, but even those who look very young to you, may well have had a number of years of experience as well as special training for the job. Not all social workers are equally knowledgeable and helpful but more and more social services departments are now appointing specialist adoption and fostering staff who rapidly acquire a great fund of experience in child placement. They may not yet have brought up a family of their own but they have probably helped many children and adopters make the big adjustments to becoming a new family. Behind the social worker who visits you lies the experience of her department and extra advice can be sought from senior social workers, from lawyers, doctors and psychiatrists.

The social workers who act as welfare supervisor and guardian *ad litem* are, of course, concerned to protect the child from unsuitable placement but they are working to protect and help you too. They will help you with any problems of adjustment that may arise and answer your questions about the adoption procedures.

These are very busy people, whose schedules are subject to frequent changes, so it may be impossible for them always to give advance notice of their visits, especially if you are not on the telephone. They will not, however, be calling unexpectedly in the hope of catching you unawares. They are quite experienced enough to see beneath the surface, and in any case are much less concerned about the appearance of your home than about the way you and your new child are settling down together. If they call at a really inconvenient moment, by all means tell them so. They will understand and try to come at another time.

In order to satisfy themselves about the suitability of the adoption and obtain the necessary information for the court, these visitors will have to ask a number of detailed and personal questions. This is not an unwarranted invasion of your privacy but an essential protection. Your replies will be kept strictly confidential and disclosed only to the court. Some of the questions may cover the same ground that you explored with the adoption agency. If this irks you, remember that the law is drawn up to protect children and parents who have not all had the benefit of placement through an approved agency.

You will discover that the more openly you can share your thoughts and feelings the more help you will receive. You will find that the health visitor is the expert on matters of baby health and feeding, the guardian *ad litem* can tell you about the court hearing, and the adoption agency visitor or local authority social worker will have experience with the problems that can so often occur when children are placed in new homes.

Your adoption agency worker is likely to be your main source of support, but use all the social workers as much as you can, for their knowledge and advice can be invaluable. You may be struggling with problems that they have met many times before. You are bound to have some moments of anxiety and there is no need to bear them alone.

# CHAPTER XI

# How and where to apply for a child

If you are in the market for a new house or a second-hand car, you have probably got a fairly good idea of how to go about finding one. Even if you have never bought a house or car yourselves, you know people who have done so, and they can give you advice on the important points to consider, snags to be avoided and what sort of service to expect from house agents or garage mechanics. Looking for a child to adopt is more difficult and sometimes it is hard to know where to start.

Some people are helped at this point by knowing another family who have successfully adopted a child through their local social services department or an adoption society. But perhaps you have heard disheartening stories about red tape, delays and searching inquiries by social workers. Very likely you question the need for this or wonder whether your home will measure up to the required standards.

There is no doubt that finding a child to adopt can be a slow, complicated and frustrating process particularly for those who are seeking one of the babies or very young children of whom there are so few. The purpose of this chapter is to provide a map and some signposts to set you on the right path. However, no matter how clear the instructions, or how hard you seek, success cannot be ensured. There are many, many more couples wanting to adopt babies than available infants. Some applicants must, inevitably, be disappointed no matter how much love and how many opportunities they can offer. If you decide to limit your application to a healthy child under 5 or 6 years old, prepare yourselves for discouragement, for a very long wait at the best and, more likely, for eventual disappointment. Even if you are

opening your hearts and home to an older or handicapped child
there can be many hurdles to overcome and long delays before
you and the child can be brought together. Just because there are
known to be dozens of youngsters of the age you want waiting for
a new family, it does not follow that any of them are in the care of
the agency to which you have applied. Even if the agency has a
child of the right age and sex, there may be several good reasons
why your home would not be the right one for this particular
child. The grafting of a child into a new family is a delicate and
highly skilled operation. If the graft is to 'take', child and family
have to be a good 'fit' and a home must be carefully selected to
meet each individual child's needs.

THE AGENCY SCENE

There is no one 'national' adoption agency even though some
societies have the word national in their title. Instead, the country is covered (more or less) with a network of adoption agencies
some of which are part of the local authority social services while
others are run by large or small voluntary organisations.

Local authorities are not yet required to act as adoption agencies. (They will be when the Children Act 1975 is fully in force.)
Most now do so, but not all, and some of those which call
themselves adoption agencies place very, very few children.

Voluntary societies providing adoption services may be large
child care organisations such as Dr Barnardo's, the National
Children's Home or The Church of England Children's Society.
All of these have regional offices in various parts of the country
but they do not cover every county. Almost all Roman Catholic
dioceses have their own adoption society catering to Catholic
children and adoptive families. Some Church of England dioceses have a church-linked adoption society though these do not
necessarily insist on church affiliation in adoptive applicants. In
some parts of the country there are local adoption societies, often
originally set up by councils of social service and in London there
are a number of voluntary organisations offering an adoption
service in the metropolitan area and home counties. It is a
confusing picture and there is no doubt that some parts of the
country are much better served than others. Depending on
where you live, you may have quite a choice of adoption agencies
or there may be only one.

Another complicating factor is that some agencies cover quite
a wide geographical area and others keep rather strictly to their

boundaries. Quite often agencies will stretch their normal geographical limits in order to find a good home for a child with
special needs, but almost none will accept 'outside' applications
from people wanting babies because they all have more than
enough applicants within their usual boundaries.

Much the best method of finding your way through this confusing scene is to write to the British Agencies for Adoption and
Fostering (address at the back of this book) and ask for their
pamphlet 'Adopting a Child'. This very inexpensive booklet is
full of information and advice. It lists all the adoption agencies in
the British Isles, tells you what geographical areas they cover,
whether they limit their work to people of a particular faith or
denomination and whether they have specific rules, e.g. about
age of applicants for babies. With this list in your hand, you can
work out which agencies you are eligible to apply to.

What the booklet cannot tell you is whether a particular
agency has any children to place at the time you want to apply or
whether their lists are closed. Because of the pressure of applications for babies, most agencies stop accepting new applicants
from time to time – indeed some lists seem to be hardly ever open
as they fill up again so quickly. The only way you can find out
about this is by writing or telephoning to inquire, but if you want
a baby there is really no point in writing to agencies that do not
cover your geographical area. (If you are a black family, most of
this does not apply as almost all adoption doors will be wide open
to you.)

For 'special needs' children, British Agencies for Adoption
and Fostering runs an Adoption Exchange Service. The
exchange exists to link children and families who may be living in
different parts of the country. Any adoption agency which is a
member of the exchange (about a hundred are) can register a
child for whom they are seeking a home or a family which is
waiting for a child. This means that a child in the care of the City
of Birmingham or one of the London boroughs could be placed
with a family on the list of an agency in Devon or Suffolk or
Durham. Over a thousand adoptive families have been brought
together through this organisation.

There are also a few agencies that specialise entirely in placing
children whose problems of health, development or adjustment
are so severe that they may never have a permanent family unless
very special efforts are made to find homes for them. The best
known of these are Barnardo's New Families Projects in Glas-
gow and Colchester, and Parents for Children in London.

HOW TO GET STARTED

If you are in the fortunate position of having a choice of possible
agencies, the first decision must be where to make your application. You will probably need to make some further inquiries.
Making an inquiry about the possibility of adoption or the sort of
children available is different from making a formal application
which always involves filling up forms and having discussions
with a social worker.

A good way of finding out more about local agencies may be
through a local group of PPIAS (Parent to Parent Information on
Adoption Services. Central address at the back of this book).
The organiser for the group in your area may have a lot of useful
advice and information to offer or you may find it helpful to talk
to couples who have experienced the agencies' services. It is well
to remember, however, that because one family has had a particularly pleasant or difficult experience with a local authority or
voluntary organisation, it does not follow that your experience
will be the same. You might be allocated a different social worker
or you might have the same worker but just be on a better (or
worse) wavelength with her. The relationship between adoptive
applicants and their social worker is bound to be quite intense
because so much is at stake on both sides. No matter how skilled
and experienced the worker may be, some people are likely to
find her (or him) more congenial than others. In this, as in so
many other aspects of adoption, there is bound to be a certain
element of luck.

In your area there may be a choice between a social services
department or a voluntary adoption society so you may wonder
which is likely to serve your needs best. There can be no overall
rule about this. On the whole, voluntary societies are smaller and
thus perhaps rather easier to deal with than the larger, more
bureaucratic local government departments. On the other hand
voluntary societies may have more rigid rules about who can be
accepted. Not many voluntary societies have children in their
own care; they are usually doing home finding for children who
are technically the responsibility of local authorities. This often
means that they are prepared to take a lot of trouble trying to link
you with a suitable child. A large social services department is
much more likely to have a suitable child in its own care, but if
there is no local child for you, their very busy social workers may
not have much time and interest in collaborating with other
agencies on your behalf. This is an aspect about which you will
have to make local inquiries.

You will probably need to find out whether the agency of your choice is accepting applications. If you are telephoning a social services department, it will be best to ask to speak to the adoptions officer. Most departments with an adoption programme of any size have an adoptions officer either at headquarters or in each area or divisional office. If you find there is no such person, it may be an indication that the department places few children for adoption. If the adoptions officer is out or busy, her secretary or clerk may be able to answer many of your questions about making an application and can tell you whether there are regular information meetings which you can attend.

By all means attend these information meetings if you have the chance. Attending will not commit you to anything. You may even want to go to meetings at more than one agency before deciding where to apply. The meetings will not only give you a 'feel' of the organisation but also enable you to find out what sort of children are available.

Some agencies may prefer that all inquiries are made by letter and in any case this may be the most convenient way for you to get in touch. When writing give your ages, occupation, religion if any, length of marriage, whether you have other children and their ages. Mention if you have adopted or fostered before and whether you have applied anywhere else. Explain the kind of child you are interested in and give the widest possible range you would consider. It is really important not to restrict your chances by setting unnecessary limits. Of course it would be pointless as well as untruthful to express an interest in a type of child you know you could never accept, and agencies understand that no one can deal with every kind of problem. Some people cannot accept physical deformity but do not mind if a child is slow at school. Others would find a slow child hard to tolerate but do not mind at all about differences in skin colour. So be honest about your major concerns but do not, for instance, limit yourselves to a baby or toddler if you feel you could stretch to a 7-year-old child. You want to start out with all your options open and if need be, you can narrow the choice down later.

If you are interested in having an older child join your family, and are writing to a social services department that does not have an adoptions officer, you may find it best to avoid the word adoption in your first letter. This is because rather few of the older children who need new families are specifically waiting to be adopted. What social services departments are often looking for are permanent foster homes which might develop into adoption. If you request an older child for adoption, some social services departments may say that they have no older children for adoption and close the door on your inquiry. What you want is an opportunity to meet a social worker and explain your hopes and wishes and the risks that you do or do not feel able to take. You must at this stage make clear your hope for eventual adoption but this may be easier in a face to face discussion than by letter. You and your social worker will need to come to an understanding about how long you are prepared to cope with the uncertainties of fostering and how you would feel about visits by the child's parents or relatives. It may be as well to have a written agreement about the plans.

Supposing you feel uncomfortable with the agency or are not able to talk easily with the social worker dealing with your application? If you have any choice of agency, it will probably be best to withdraw gracefully at this point. The social worker may suggest this herself if she feels things are not going well or your application is unlikely to be accepted. If possible, you want to avoid an outright rejection as this may stand in the way of your applying somewhere else. If you withdraw of your own accord, are still sure that you have something good to offer a child and are not limiting yourselves to a young, healthy white baby, it is well worth starting again with another agency. But if this should happen several times, you may just have to recognise that there could be something wrong which you cannot see at present but which would prevent a happy outcome to an adoption.

RED TAPE AND THE REASONS FOR IT

The work of adoption agencies is rather closely defined by laws and official regulations whose purpose is to ensure that everyone's rights are properly safeguarded. The Children Act 1975 decreed that individuals should no longer be allowed to place children for adoption. Children need to be protected from unnecessary separation from their original families as well as from unsuitable placements. Natural parents need protection against hasty or ill-thought out decisions and adoptive applicants should be safeguarded against unnecessary risks. They have a right to be given all available information about any known or discoverable physical or mental handicaps, serious behaviour problems or risks of inheritance.

To provide these safeguards agencies are required to make all sorts of inquiries and reports. The child and the prospective adopters must be medically examined, police and local authority health checks must be made and references taken up. Every placement must be approved by an adoption case committee or panel that has power to reject applications from people considered unsuitable in any way. The committee or panel is not required to give reasons for its decisions though many will do so.

A good adoption agency will do much more than merely comply with the law. The social worker will want to get to know you very thoroughly indeed. You and she are going to have to do a lot of very hard thinking and straight talking together.

Perhaps you will feel a little uncomfortable and resentful about this at first because it is not easy to allow a stranger to know the intimate details of one's life and feelings. But when you think of it, if your child were being placed for adoption you would want very thorough inquiries to be made and if the study of you and your home is full and careful, then you can be confident that equally careful work is likely to be done in studying and preparing the child.

The social worker's job is to help you decide whether you truly want to become the parents of an adopted child and, if so, what sort of child. She has to satisfy herself that you are likely to be able to carry out your plans successfully. She has to know you well enough to be able to suggest a suitable child to you or, if you are interested in a child who has been advertised as needing a family, she has to help you to decide whether you and this child will really be a good 'match'. Then she has to help you with any difficulties that arise while the child is settling into your family. If you are taking a child past infancy, this last part is particularly important as your social worker's support and advice may be crucial to the success of the placement.

The adoption of older children is very similar to marriage and the role of the social worker is in many cases not unlike that of the 'go-between' or 'match-maker' in an arranged marriage. For a successful outcome, this role requires tact, sensitivity and a sound understanding of human nature.

ADVERTISING CHILDREN

The idea of advertising children in need of homes is at first sight rather distasteful and when the first youngsters appeared on TV there was a storm of protest. But it soon became clear that advertising works. The children are sensible and generous enough to be willing to speak for others as well as themselves and are unharmed by the experience. Hundreds have now found homes through publicity of various kinds. It is also a great help to would-be adopters and foster parents to see pictures and have details of the kinds of children who are needing new families.

If you join PPIAS (see above) you will receive a regular newsletter which carries photographs and descriptions of waiting children. As you would expect, these are children with very special needs. Many are slow learners, have behaviour problems, many are black, have been in children's homes or hospitals for many years or have serious medical problems. Others are normal youngsters but in family groups of three or more brothers and sisters who want to stay together.

The *Be My Parent* book is a new development. It is a loose-leaf book with pictures and descriptions of waiting children and it is kept constantly up to date so that you can tell if a particular child is already being considered by another family. PPIAS organisers and member agencies of the BAAF Exchange Service all have copies of *Be My Parent* so you can ask to see it any time. It is also in some local libraries.

Looking over lists of children each with his or her own problems, hopes and fears can be a rather overwhelming experience. You may feel you would like to help all of them or you may feel that the difficulties they present are just too great. It could be that you find yourselves quickly and irresistibly drawn to a particular child. More likely, you will need to look at the book or newsletter several times gradually sorting out your ideas, getting used to the way the children are described and learning to read between the lines of the short descriptions of personality and behaviour. It may not be that you find your child through this method but through discussing a particular child you can learn a lot about adoption in general. Books and lists of this sort will give you great food for thought and will help you to sort out your ideas and find out about the various kinds of problems or handicaps that the waiting children face.

You just might meet your future child at an adoption party. The growth of adoption parties is another imaginative scheme to help parentless children and childless couples get together. These are genuine social events where adults and children go to meet each other and have fun, but they also have a serious underlying purpose.

Children who may doubt the possibility of having new parents are helped by seeing some flesh and blood people who want a child. Would-be adopters who find it hard to imagine what the waiting children are really like, find that it stimulates their thinking and planning if they can meet, play and share a meal with actual youngsters who want families. People sometimes find themselves attracted to a child very different from their expectations. Some very happy adoptions have started at an adoption party, but since it is rather a new idea, you may not get the chance to go to one.

# CHAPTER XII

# Preparing to be parents

Not knowing when the 'happy event' will take place is one of the hard things about being an adoptive parent. Even after your application is approved by the agency's case committee and your name is on the waiting list, no one can say for sure just when the right child will become available. Even if you have asked for a particular child from a list of waiting children, it will take time to complete the necessary formalities and you may have to accept the disappointment of learning that another home has been selected as being an even better 'fit' than yours.

Waiting is difficult. At first one is buoyed up with excitement and anticipation but after a time this fades. Waiting makes people feel helpless and angry. The prospect of becoming a parent no longer seems real. It is easy to feel that the agency has forgotten you and is not interested in your needs. Nothing can make the waiting period easy but you can do some things to make it a useful, constructive period. And it may help a little to reflect on how much more difficult it must be for a child, desperate for a family of his own and also dependent on 'the system' to find him new parents.

It will not do any harm to write or telephone the agency occasionally reminding them of your deep interest in having a child. If you decide that you can stretch your ideas and take one older than you had originally decided, or if you have had an idea about fixing the attic into another bedroom so you could now take a brother and sister, by all means tell them so. But it does no good, and may do harm, to pester or badger your social worker. She cannot just order a suitable child from a shop for you. Once again, your best source of support is likely to be your local adoptive parents group where you will meet people who have been through the process before as well as others in the same uncomfortable predicament.

## WAITING FOR A FIRST BABY

During the nine months of pregnancy husbands and wives have an opportunity to get accustomed to the fact that a baby will be born to them. The baby is obviously a real, live human being even before he is born. Then, too, Nature usually prepares a mother emotionally for this new experience and her feelings change and develop with the gradual changes in her body.

A mother through adoption is no less a mother, but her pregnancy is different. Because there are no physical changes associated with waiting for an adopted child, she will have to make a special effort to think herself into the role of mother. Besides, she has two tasks, not just one. She has not only to get used to the idea that she will have a child but she must also try to make sure that she has faced and accepted the fact that this child will not come to her in the usual way.

Enlarging your family circle from two to three will mean making some adjustments in your relationships as well as in your routines. You might use this time to understand each other more fully and talk through your plans for parenthood and how you will work together to achieve a truly happy family. Do not expect too much of yourselves too soon. Everyone takes time to learn to be a parent and some things can only be learned as you and your children live together.

As well as this emotional preparation there may be many practical things to be done in your home during the waiting period. You can enjoy getting a bedroom suitably decorated and furnished and you may like to get on with other jobs around the house so as to have more time for the baby when he comes. Of course it is a temptation to go out and buy all kinds of baby clothes and equipment, but it would be wiser to put money aside each week. Then when you know for sure about your child's age and size, you can go out and buy what you need very quickly. It is surprising how much you can borrow, too, especially baby things which are only needed for a few months and then sit in the attic for years.

Unless you have already had a good deal of experience with babies it is as well to get some now. Watch a friend bath and dress her baby and then ask if you can try it a few times. Offer to baby-sit for her and put the children to bed. Practise making up a milk formula and feeding a baby with a bottle and with a spoon. It is not quite as simple as it looks. Such little details as the heat of the bath water or when to stop feeding for wind can cause anxiety to the uninitiated, not to speak of the problems of pinning a nappie on to a wriggling, screaming baby or lifting a slippery, soapy little body into the bath! It is a big help if you have learned to feel comfortable and relaxed when handling a baby because then the baby will feel comfortable and relaxed too.

One young couple adopting 8-month-old Nicholas spent a most miserable first twenty-four hours. Nicholas was shy and frightened. He cried all the way home and they could not persuade him to eat any cereal at supper-time. He drank a little milk but cried most of the night while they walked the floor with him. They were sure he must be hungry but he ate almost no breakfast. More tears followed during the morning. In desperation they went to see the husband's sister, who had three little children. The family was just finishing lunch and there was blancmange on the table. The sister took Nicky from his exhausted new mother and, almost automatically, began putting spoonfuls of blancmange into his rapidly opening mouth. His parents looked on amazed. Nicholas would not open his mouth for them.

Finally they realised that in their fear of hurting him they had gingerly put the spoon to his lips instead of on to his tongue. Nicky sensed an unsure hand and was frightened. He never got the food into his mouth in such a way that he could swallow it comfortably. After this hurdle was over the new family settled down quite happily, but a little baby practise could have spared them a bad start.

Many infant welfare clinics and some adoption agencies run courses for new mothers and sometimes for new fathers too. It might be a good idea to call at the clinic and inquire about classes and discussion groups. You could also get acquainted with the health visitor who will be visiting you when your child arrives.

DO SOME READING AND MAKE SOME CONTACTS

No one can learn to be a good parent just from reading books. It takes practise too. On the other hand, lack of knowledge and trial-and-error methods can be hard on both parent and child.

The most helpful books are not the ones that give detailed instructions about what to do, but the ones which help you to understand how a child feels, thinks and grows. Once you have a working knowledge of children's physical and emotional development and what can be expected at different ages, then you can make some decisions for yourselves on how to bring up your family. There is no one perfect method and no rules will fit every child and every occasion. Good parents are flexible and never stop learning.

It is easy to get unnecessarily worried if you do not know whether your child's behaviour is usual or unusual for his age. Is it a sign of a vicious temperament if an 8-month-old baby bites his mother? Do most 2-year-olds wet the bed? Is it stealing when a boy of 4 brings his friend's toy truck home with him? Will he really become insane or immoral if he masturbates a good deal? These are questions which most parents ask at one time or another and they need answers before they can know whether to be upset and punish or consider the incident an ordinary and inevitable part of growing up.

There are many very good books on child care which will give some answers. Your doctor, the health visitor or your local librarian can offer suggestions. There is a danger, however, in reading too many since different authors do have different theories and this can be confusing. It is better to read and digest one or two you feel you can trust. It helps to have one handy in times of stress. One adoptive mother tells how the first time her little daughter had a real temper tantrum she rushed to her baby 'bible' for advice. By the time she had read the relevant paragraph the tantrum was over!

If you are white and planning to adopt a black child, the waiting time can be useful for making contacts in the black community, getting tips from black mothers on how to deal with a black child's hair and skin (special grooming is really necessary), and finding out where you can get black dolls and children's books which show youngsters of all races. Black children often find that they cannot identify with any character in an 'all-white' book, so may end up feeling that books are not for them. There are now books with multi-racial pictures such as the familiar nursery rhymes with up-dated pictures in Puffin's *Mother Goose comes to Cable Street*.

There is a valuable organisation called Harmony which you may well want to join. Harmony members are people of all races with many multi-racial families through mixed marriages, adoption and fostering. They are people committed to the idea of a multi-racial society. There are local groups, a newsletter with helpful articles and lists of suitable children's books. Harmony's central address is listed at the end of this book.

## WAITING FOR AN OLDER CHILD

If yours is to be an older child adoption, you will not have to worry about learning the practical aspects of baby care. But you will be well advised to learn all you can about the development and behaviour of young children as well as those of the age you expect the newcomer to be. Understanding the normal development of young children can be a real practical help to parents grappling with the behaviour problems inevitably experienced in older child placements. Behaviour which at first sight seems extraordinary may just be occurring at an inappropriate age. You can get books on child development from your public libary.

Rare indeed is the older child who needs new parents and has not experienced many emotionally damaging experiences. Your new child's emotional development will almost certainly have been stunted in some respects and precociously forced in others. He may have just had his ninth birthday, but sometimes he will act like a 12-year-old and at others, more frequently, like a 7-year-old, a 4-year-old or even a toddler in a tantrum. If you have a good grasp of the normal stages of development you will be able to understand how emotional damage or blocks at certain stages result in particular behaviour problems such as over-eating or messy habits. The babyish behaviour your 9-year-old puts on some days will be easier to tolerate if you realise that he is only going back and catching up on stages which he missed or in which his development took a wrong turning and needs straightening out.

Children joining new families are often adept at playing adults off against one another so, as far as humanly possible, you are going to need a united approach. Think ahead about your priorities and what matters most. Discuss rules, every family must have some, and talk about discipline and punishments. You cannot and should not set up rigid expectations for yourselves or the child, but by sharing your thoughts and feelings you can understand each other's point of view and make sure that you agree on the basics. And on smaller but pressing matters: are you going to allow unlimited TV? What about bedtimes, pocket money, helping with the washing-up?

A new child in the family is going to create work, occupy time and make big demands on your energy. You will almost certainly have to change some of your routines and thinking this through in advance may help. Are there ways in which household chores could be simplified? Would it be possible to invest in a tumble drier so that wet beds do not pose a major problem? What about storage space for clothes, toys, a bike? All adoptive parents need time off for themselves and you will want to find a mature and reliable baby-sitter.

If you do not normally have much contact with children, you may realise that you have forgotten the stories, songs and games of your childhood. Now is the time to refresh your memory. Especially when you are first getting to know your child, you will need some things to do together. Knowing a few paper and pencil games, some simple card games with 'I spy' and its variants to play in the car will all help to break the ice and aid in getting acquainted.

Another piece of preparatory work is to think ahead to how you are going to present yourselves and your home to the forth-coming member of the family. A useful tool in this process is a specially prepared photograph album or scrap-book. You can give this to the social worker to help her prepare the child for the meeting or you can give it to him yourselves to help him begin to understand what it would be like to join your family and to make it all seem real in between the introductory visits. It is probably best not to put the book together until you have information about a particular child because you will want to make it personal and geared to his age and interests. But looking out suitable snapshots and getting copies made, buying an inexpensive album or scrap-book and thinking ahead about what might be included will enable you to put it together quickly when the time comes. Leave some blank pages at the end for photographs of you all together as a new family.

Of course you will be giving thought to where your new child will sleep. To have a room of his own may be a special thrill to a child who has lived in group care. (It can also be a bit scary at night.) You will want to find a balance between advance prepara-tions which make the room seem ready and welcoming and allowing the child to share in the choice of colour schemes, painting and fixing.

Look around your house and garden with the child's needs in mind. If you are considering a child with a physical handicap you may need to consider minor adaptations such as ramps and rails. A mentally handicapped child will have little sense of danger so garden gates and fences may be particularly important.

If you have not already looked into the question of suitable schools, now is the time to do so. In this and so many other matters it will help a lot to talk to parents of other children and learn from their experience. Your child may have different needs from theirs, but talking about the possibilities and pitfalls will help you think yourself into your new role.

## IF YOU ARE ADDING TO THE FAMILY

If you are parents already, many of the things we have been discussing in this chapter will not apply and the practical aspects of caring for a child will usually present no problems. You will, however, have another important job to do in preparing your present child (or children) for a new brother or sister. The importance of this cannot be over-emphasised.

Additions of babies or older children bring different problems. Let's consider babies first.

If you are waiting for a baby or toddler you very likely have only one child who is quite young himself. It will be difficult or impossible for him to imagine what having a baby in the home will really be like. Even when he has been begging for a baby brother for years he may suggest after a few days that you send the baby back. Such jealousy is neither wicked nor unusual. In fact, it would be abnormal for a child to feel no twinge of jealousy at any time, even if he does not show it openly. Most children feel a mixture of love, pride, jealousy and dislike. After all, it is not easy to move gracefully from being the centre of attention and to see one's place as the favoured youngest taken by a stranger. Most children have a secret longing to be the best-loved child and feel threatened by a new baby. Well-meaning friends and relatives do not help when they arrive with presents for the baby and hang over the pram with the exclamations of pleasure that used to be reserved for your elder child, while he looks sadly on from outside the charmed circle. It is often a good idea to lay in a nice present for the elder child to receive from the new brother or sister.

If your first child is adopted he will need especially sensitive understanding, for his place in the family is not quite so secure. Even if he was much too little to have any conscious memory of his natural mother, the fact remains that every adopted child has had at least one change of home and often more than one. Children vary, of course, and your child may take the newcomer in his stride. But do not count on this or be surprised if it does not happen.

Just as you have missed the physical preparation of pregnancy, so for your elder child the idea of a new member of the household is very unreal. You cannot tell him just when it will happen and he does not see you getting bigger and growing the baby. Time means little to a child, and if you have been waiting for some months he may give up hope. Larry, a 5-year-old, announced that he was not going to pray to God for a baby sister any more because God obviously did not listen to his prayers.

How much you tell your child will depend on his age. If he is still only a toddler, it may be wisest to say very little until you are sure your adoption application has been accepted. If he is older, the adoption agency will want to know his views. In either case, when you start making preparations, let him help. Let him feel that you are doing this all together as a family and that his contribution is important. As soon as you know the age of your new child give your youngster some idea of what he can expect. An infant can be a disappointment to a child who has longed for a companion. 'Why, it's only a toy baby!' said one little boy in disgust. On the other hand, an inquisitive toddler who pokes into cupboards, breaks dolls and tears precious books can be a real trial to a little girl who has hoped for a baby she can help look after. Neither of these situations needs to be bad if it is expected and planned for.

Try not to make big changes in your first child's life just when the new baby comes. If he starts school just then he may feel he is unwanted at home and is being pushed out. If he has to give up his cot for the baby he may resent it. Going to school or having a big bed will be pleasurable and exciting if it is part of growing up and not associated with losing his place as only child.

In some ways it is easier to prepare an older child for a newcomer, but when the new member of the family will himself be 'older' the preparation is difficult because you cannot know quite what to expect. What you can be sure about, however, is that there will be times the old and new children do not get along, when quarrels flare up and family tensions are high. There will be times when the new child wishes he had not come and times when your existing children fervently wish the new addition would go back where he came from. Foreseeing these hurt, angry feelings and reassuring everyone that this is normal and natural may help a bit. Your present children need to realise that love and understanding between them and the newcomer will grow gradually and that whatever happens their place in the family is secure and your love for them unfaltering. Try to help them be as realistic as possible in their expectations and help them to realise that the new child's behaviour and interests may be different from theirs, especially at first.

# CHAPTER XIII

# Preparing children for new families

While you are getting yourselves ready for the addition of a new member of the family, somewhere a social worker will be preparing your child for this frightening and painful step into the future.

The suggestion that coming to your home will be frightening and painful may be rather shocking when you know how much love is waiting there and how warm the welcome will be. But it is important to remember the child's side of things. It is true that in the long run he is going to gain a great deal from the move, but for the present there will also be loss and the grief of partings. He will have to leave the familiar and venture alone into the unknown. If the past has been full of unpleasant and confusing experiences, he will have little confidence that the future really holds something good. Even if he wants a mummy and daddy very much, there are no doubt certain people in his present life that he is fond of and will not want to leave. He may indeed be deeply attached to his present housemother or temporary foster parents and it may be difficult for him to understand why he has to move. Explaining this and helping the child to understand the difference between his present situation and a 'forever' family where he can grow up is one of the most challenging and important of an adoption worker's tasks.

Getting a child ready to move into a new family involves a lot more than packing his clothes and toys. There is another form of luggage to be packed in the form of information about his past and about his present life, his likes and dislikes, behaviour and health. Above all, the child himself must be got ready mentally and emotionally as well as physically. The older the child, the greater the amount of work to be done, but even babies have their personal luggage.

The law requires that every child who is placed for adoption should be medically examined. In addition, the agency must provide adoptive parents with a health history which should include details of birth, developmental milestones, immunisations and information about any illnesses or accidents and about the natural family's health.

For older children an educational history is also important with details of schools attended, reports of progress and information about special achievements, interests or learning problems. It is helpful to know how the child has appeared to his teachers and how he has got along with other children at school. Is he popular or a bit of a loner?

One of the ways to ease the change, especially for babies and young children, is to make as few alterations in their routines as possible. This means that the social worker and the child's present caretakers will need to provide you with a very detailed description of daily routines, food, toys, sleep patterns and usual activities. It is crucial to have a note of the words a toddler uses for bed, bath, pot, drink etc., what he calls his present caretakers or the members of his family, whether he has a security blanket or other 'precious object' and what he calls it.

If the social worker does not provide this sort of information, you must be sure to obtain it for yourselves from the child's foster parents or housemother or, if you are not going to meet them, insist that the social worker get these details for you. Knowing these things will be vital to your child's comfort and to your peace of mind, especially during the early days of his life with you.

THE CHILD'S NEED TO UNDERSTAND

Good preparation for family placement always means making the move less frightening and painful but when an older child is involved it also means something more. The move is a watershed in the child's life and it provides an opportunity to help him come to terms with his past. It is a time when he can be helped to understand who he is, where he came from and why things have happened as they have.

We are frequently tempted to avoid talking about painful matters. People often say that children's memories are short and that it is better not to upset them by talking about the past. This is a very, very serious mistake when it comes to adoption and has caused untold misery and problems.

Before a child can build a sound future he must settle his past so that it can provide a secure foundation for growth. As any gardener knows, flowers and vegetables only flourish when their roots are securely planted in the soil. Children are the same. If they have to try to develop from a life base of confusion or uncertainty their emotional growth is likely to be stunted or distorted.

Dealing with the past is a crucial part of a successful adoption placement. It is difficult and frequently takes time. Often it will not be fully completed before the child joins his new family so it may well be up to you to continue this very important piece of work.

Little children are apt to be very muddled about what causes things to happen. They do not understand the difference between magic and reality and often believe that what they wish for will actually happen. So if he has been very angry with a parent who then dies or goes away, the young child is likely to think it was his fault and that he worked a 'bad magic'. Children often carry a tremendous burden of guilt because they think that by their thoughts or behaviour they have caused their parent's illness, divorce or desertion. Adults do not help by comments like, 'You'll be the death of me' or 'If you do that again I'll have you put away.'

It is an unfortunate reality that children in care often have to move several times in the course of a few years. Simon's case is fairly typical. He came into care when his parents were evicted from their council house for non-payment of rent. At that point it was hoped that the family would be reunited so, after a couple of weeks in a reception centre, Simon, aged 4, went to short-stay foster parents. Unfortunately Simon's own family's situation deteriorated rather than improved. His father committed a serious offence in a desperate attempt to restore the family fortunes and received a long prison sentence. His mother 'went to pieces', stopped visiting Simon and then found a new man friend and left the district. When the short-stay foster parents could not keep him any more, Simon was moved to another foster home and then to a children's home. This made four moves in less than a year and by this time he was very mixed up, unhappy and difficult. He had often been naughty at home and had moved back and forth between his parents and a grandmother who had since died. Now he felt that the loss of his parents was because he was a bad boy and they did not love him any more. The moves from the two foster homes only served to reinforce this idea but of course he could not put all these feelings into words.

Simon's social worker and his foster parents and housemother all recognised that he was unhappy but just accepted this as an inevitable result of what had happened. People were kind to him and tried to tolerate his often intolerable behaviour. No one really tried to help this child with his overwhelming feelings of guilt, distress and confusion. An attempt to place him with long-term foster parents broke down after eight months because Simon could not seem to accept them or show any affectionate response. What was urgently needed was someone with the skill and understanding to help this little boy to unravel the tangled threads of his past and get it into perspective. He needed help to see that his parents had grown-up problems, so they could not manage their lives very well or take care of children but that these problems were nothing to do with Simon himself.

## LIFE-STORY BOOKS

A very successful way of helping children like Simon to make sense of their family background and their own life experience is making what is called a life-story book. This is something like the baby books which some families keep but much more individual. In a scrap-book or album, the child and social worker together write the story of the child's life including information about his original family. It is illustrated with photographs, drawings and pictures from magazines. How much is written by the social worker and how much written or dictated by the child will vary, but the youngster's full participation is always important. To start with, a child may resist either openly or subtly saying that he doesn't want to remember, but the attraction of choosing a scrap-book and working with paints, crayons and glue usually helps to get over the beginning hurdles. There may be painful times dealing with sad or hurtful memories, but in the end children get immense satisfaction out of their books.

Whenever possible, the social worker or houseparent will try to track down and collect pictures of people and places that have been part of the child's life and photos of the child himself at different ages. This often requires a good deal of time and effort but is time well spent. It is a real deprivation not to know what one looked like as a baby, to have no pictures of one's parents, to be confused about one's relationship to people vaguely remembered from the past.

The purpose of all this is not to re-awaken the child's interest in his natural parents or revive his hopes of returning to them. Just the opposite. The objective is to make it possible for the child to put the past behind him, to enable him to stop thinking about it so much and to concentrate on the present and future. While there are mysteries in the past, unspoken hopes and fears, muddled memories and missing bits no child can be fully at ease with himself.

Because a child in care does not talk about the past, we should not assume that he does not think a lot about it. A great many children in care suffer from a serious lack of concentration which is a great handicap to their progress at school. Not only do they day-dream during lessons, they often have very little intellectual energy for learning or even for creative hobbies. One of the main reasons for this is their pre-occupation with trying to make sense of what has happened to them and why. Like Leslie who could not read till he found out what had happened to his mother, they have to be freed from this burden before they can make progress.

YOUR PART IS IMPORTANT TOO

It could happen that you take into your home a child whose social worker has not done much to explain or deal with his past. Or it may be that this task has been well started but is not yet completed. In some instances, you and the social worker may decide that it would be best for you to help make a life-story book with your child. Certainly working together on such a book is an excellent way of building and deepening a relationship. Closeness is developed by sharing both pleasurable and painful memories, by going together to visit places the child has lived in or perhaps a cemetery where a loved relative is buried. Writing to former houseparents or foster parents to ask for photographs, records and mementos provides opportunity to talk and learn about the child's recollections and feelings. And actually putting the material into the book can be a shared enterprise in which adult and child use their artistic skills and imagination to produce something attractive and satisfying. Do remember, however, that the life-story book is a tool rather than an end in itself. It is more important that the child feel satisfied and involved than that the book look perfect or be absolutely complete.

Whether you work on the life-story book yourself or only see one that was made before you came into the picture, you will find it an invaluable aid to increasing your knowledge and understanding of your child, his behaviour, and his attitudes to life and people. Over the years you will find the book a useful tool for explaining adoption and it will help to open up the subject of the original parents. Your own preparation of yourself in coming to terms with realities will now prove its worth.

It is always hard for adoptive parents to feel that they have missed out on a part of their child's life. The album can help you toward some sense of participation. Then too, learning in detail about difficult periods in your child's life may provide clues to where and why he has got stuck at a certain stage of development. When you understand this you will be able to give extra help to overcome the block to progress.

There will be encouraging things in the record also. One of the benefits of a good life-story book is that it provides an opportunity to emphasise the positive aspects of the story, the good relationships, the happy events and special achievements. Cards sent from friends and relatives show that one was valued and not forgotten. Train tickets may recall an exciting journey. A certificate for third prize in the egg and spoon race at school sports may not in itself be a major landmark, but to a youngster whose life story offers little to be proud of, it is a memory to be cherished and built upon. One little success can create confidence for further efforts.

# CHAPTER XIV

# Meeting your new child

Anyone who tells you that he or she went through the experience of adopting a child without a qualm is fooling himself and you.

When at long last you hear by letter or telephone that a child is available you will no doubt expect to feel only the most radiant happiness and excitement. Do not be too surprised, however, if the first thing you do is to burst into tears, or if amid the pleasure you have moments of real fear and anxiety. Part of this is a reaction to the strain and tension of waiting, part an increased realisation of the true meaning of adoption, and part a quite natural hesitation in the face of such an important decision and responsibility. As one very capable and warm-hearted woman who was going to adopt twins said, 'Twenty-three hours a day I feel this is the most wonderful thing that ever happened to me. The twenty-fourth hour I think I must be mad!'

Some people are naturally more nervous than others, but butterflies in the stomach, weakness at the knees and a lump in the throat are common experiences. Of course you feel happy and thrilled and of course you want a child very much, but no doubt you have a few fears too and it is no good pretending they do not exist. If you stuff them down inside and feel ashamed and guilty they are likely to rise up again with renewed strength – perhaps just at the moment you are meeting your child and when you most want to be free to give your full attention to him. It is far better to look at your doubts in advance, air them, share them and then accept them as a natural but passing phase.

The length of time between hearing about a child and meeting him can vary from a day or so to several weeks. If a baby is being placed direct from a maternity hospital, the arrangements will all have to be made very quickly. In fact it may all seem quite a rush, particularly if you have been waiting a long time with nothing apparently happening. But if you are going to be introduced to an older or 'special needs' child, things will probably move more slowly especially if the child is in the care of another agency in a different part of the country. The co-ordination of arrangements for meetings and pre-placement visits can be complicated and time consuming.

Whatever the time span, there are usually several definite stages:

1   News of an available child.
2   Detailed information about the child, his personal situation and needs.
3   A first meeting with the child.
4   Introductory visits.
5   The child comes to live with you.

Having heard by letter or telephone that the agency has a child they feel you will be interested in, you will have an opportunity to learn more about him in a meeting with your social worker. If the child has a different social worker, you will very likely meet him or her too. This is a very important stage because now, for the first time, you will have really detailed information about a child who may join your family. If yours is to be an older child, the social worker will probably have photographs to show you and through sharing information from the child's present caretakers, she will try to give you a full and realistic picture of his present health, behaviour and abilities and what his life experiences have been. She will also tell you something about his first parents, how they feel about the adoption plan and whether there are likely to be any legal complications. Some agencies allow parents to read all or part of the child's file at some stage.

It can be difficult to take in all this information at once but do not worry as you will have chances to go over it again. You may feel scared by the prospect of a real child after so much talking and dreaming. You may feel it is still all a dream. If you find yourself reacting really negatively to what you learn, and the child being suggested does not seem right for you, by all means feel free to express your doubts or even to decide there and then that this youngster will not be suited to your family. While you certainly do not want to turn down a child just because you have a moment of panic, it could happen that the agency has misunderstood your feelings or expectations and is making an inappropriate suggestion. It could even be that when it comes right to the point, either now or at the first meeting with the child, that you find that you do not want to go through with an adoption plan at all. This has happened to quite a lot of people along the way. Though you may find it very painful, little or no harm will be done if you withdraw now and the social worker will respect your honesty.

Even if you feel rather certain that you want to move ahead and meet the child you have been hearing about, you will almost certainly be asked to go home and sleep on the decision for at least one night. There is such a lot to think about at this stage and you must not rush ahead blindly for too much is at stake.

## THE FIRST MEETING

There is no one right way to manage the delicate manoeuvre of transferring a child from one home to another, so each placement has to be planned individually.

If you already have children, you will need to think carefully about whether or not to take them with you for the first meeting. There can be no hard and fast rule, but experience seems to show that it is often best if the father and mother go alone. They are the ones who have to make the decision about whether to go ahead. Also, they will want to give full attention to the new child and this may be difficult if their own children are shy or showing off or needing reassurance.

Where and how you first meet will depend on the agency's policy, the child's age and his present situation. The most usual meeting place is a foster home or children's home but it could be an office, a hospital or in a public place like a zoo or café. Your social worker will know what will be most appropriate for your child and she will probably also have ideas about whether it would be appropriate to take along a small present for an older child and, if so, what to take for him.

While some couples are fortunate enough to feel certain about their new child right from the start, others find the first meeting an unexpectedly upsetting experience.

A mother who had two sons by birth and then adopted a baby girl, wrote about it later:

> To me, having had babies the natural and supposedly hard
> way, this form of delivery was far more confusing and almost
> as painful! I could hardly breathe as I heard the nurse coming

down the stairs. In another instant the baby was in my arms.
. . . Volumes couldn't compass the thoughts that engulfed me
as I held our new baby all the long drive back. I was proud
and terrified and confident and amazed – all the sensations of
a new mother but every one of them different from any I had
known before.

Just occasionally, uncertainties become difficulties which can
reach major proportions and may be a sign that either husband or
wife unconsciously does not really want a child or perhaps that
they need more time to get used to the idea. Unexplained attacks
of vomiting, indigestion, severe headaches, persistent sleepless-
ness and even temporary paralysis are some of the symptoms that
give warning all is not well and that placement of the child should
be at least delayed.

Though such acute upsets are rare and serious, more minor
ones are quite common and can be the prelude to an entirely
happy and successful adoption. Experience seems to show that
parents who have lost a child through death may find this introduction a particularly difficult moment because sometimes they
are unconsciously expecting to see a child just like their own.
When they do not, the feeling of difference can be a shock which
it takes time to get over.

Sometimes, too, people find that they just do not take to the
child they are first offered. This is, of course, more likely to
happen if the child you go to meet is very different from the sort
of child you originally had in mind or is handicapped in some way
or well beyond the appealing infant and toddler stage.

It can be surprisingly difficult to know how one does feel after
a first meeting. The child may seem quite different from the
photographs. (They were probably taken some months ago and
children change fast.) The handicap may seem worse than you
expected. After so much anxious expectation you may now feel
quite numb. Certainly you are most unlikely to feel instant love –
love takes time to grow. It may come to one partner more quickly
than another. In older child placements, you probably cannot
hope to feel more than liking and some degree of attraction or
interest at first. Even these may only come gradually. The danger
signals are not lack of love but an active feeling of dislike or
repugnance or an immediate wish to change a lot of things about
the child. Of course there will be aspects of his appearance,
speech, behaviour and manners which could do with improvement. But your acceptance of a child cannot be on the basis that

some things about him must change. You need to be able to take him into your family as he is and let any changes come gradually. If you feel that he needs to be 'made over', then draw back. It will be much better for him to wait for another family where he will fit in more easily.

## THE CHILD'S POINT OF VIEW

Although the main purpose of this first meeting is to enable you to test your own reactions, it is also an immensely important moment for the child. He, too, has to adjust his dream parents to the reality that is you.

Occasionally it may be thought best for potential adopters to have an opportunity to see an older or handicapped child without his realising who they are. The aim, of course, is to protect his feelings if the couple do not take to him, but there is always the risk that an alert child will guess anyway and perhaps feel he is being deceived. More often, the child's own social worker will have been talking with him about you, perhaps showing him your family album and generally preparing him to move.

If the child is less than a year old or is mentally handicapped, not much preparatory work can be done ahead of the first meeting. But when this moment comes, it is essential that every child play his full part in the proceedings. The capacity of even a very tiny child to do this can be truly amazing.

What we want to avoid is the feeling of 'being done to'. Many children being placed for adoption have had experiences of abrupt changes of home. They have been moved about like parcels without proper explanation or an opportunity to express their wishes and views. It is crucial that this last move be different. The child has to be helped to take on his new parents at his own speed and in his own way. He certainly needs to know that this is a plan which his social worker has made because she believes it is right for him and that important people in his life give their approval. He will also need the supporting help of the new parents, who will show that they love and want him. But they cannot go all the way to the child – he must also make some move towards them and show his readiness to accept them. A school-age child will be able to ask questions, make comments and explain at least some of his feelings. Younger children and babies cannot explain themselves in words and have to show us how they feel by their actions and expressions. One has to be alert to their individual methods of communication.

Terry was 15 months old and a very shy, sensitive child who would cling to his foster mother and cry at the sight of strangers. It seemed that moving to an adoption home would be very hard for him, but it was necessary. His new parents, Ian and Joan Hurst, were warm, intelligent and sympathetic. They agreed to move slowly in their introduction to Terry and planned to see him several times before taking him home with them.

The meetings went off better than anyone had dared to hope. At first Terry cried and was frightened; he clung to his foster mother and social worker. Gradually he became more friendly, was able to play a little, accepted the gift of a toy duck and even kissed Ian and Joan goodbye. At each visit Terry gained confidence and understanding. His social worker and foster mother told him in simple words about the new house and the new bed, the brown dog and, above all, the new mummy and daddy. Terry listened with an occasional sob and an increasing grasp of the situation. Ian and Joan confessed to the social worker afterwards that they had not believed it would be possible for so young a child to understand what was happening, but they were convinced by what they saw and heard. After several visits, including a whole day which the Hursts spent in the foster home, Terry was able to go with them calmly and happily. He enjoyed his new family from the first, and from being a shy, timid baby, became a friendly confident little boy.

If a child is to understand what is happening in an adoption placement he must be helped to realise that the meeting with the prospective adopters is not just a social occasion but something much more important. This will be mainly up to the social worker, but adopters can help too by their own understanding of what is involved and their willingness to let the child express his feelings and move at his own pace.

Change and newness are frightening. Because of his limited understanding and lack of experience, a little child can only cope with relatively few events at any one time. But thoughtful study and long experience have shown social workers that a child can stand quite painful changes if they come to him in little pieces. He can accept one thing at a time, whereas the complete experience would be overwhelming. Thus, the timing of a move for a child is of particular importance.

Some adults find this hard to accept. They are still inclined to act on the assumption that because babies cannot talk and explain themselves they either have no feelings or cannot understand. So plans are imposed on them. These people will pay careful attention to the wishes and feelings of the adopters but will hand over a small, sensitive person as though he were a bag of groceries. Of course one reason for this attitude is that it is easier. It saves trouble and it saves facing the fact that babies and children suffer when they have to change homes – even when they go to homes where they are much loved and wanted. It is easier to pretend that the baby does not notice and to say the child will soon get over it. He probably will, but there is no reason for increasing his suffering and confusion by thoughtlessness or indifference. We must use our imagination, knowledge and understanding to help a child move from security into an unknown world.

Most mothers recognise this instinctively as they teach their children to do without them for a while. The wise mother will be away only a short time when she first leaves her toddler with a neighbour or baby-sitter. She will explain before she goes that she will be back very soon, and she keeps her word. Gradually she will extend her absences so that her child can be left for a day, and by degrees for a week-end, with someone he knows and trusts.

In the same way a child being placed for adoption needs to learn to separate himself from one familiar person or place before he can take on another. How long this takes will depend on his age, his life experience and his temperament. Quite often a child is unable to accept both new parents at the same time. If he can warm up to one of them at the first meeting, adopters should feel well-satisfied.

It is not unknown for a child to reject new parents and feel they are not people he wants to live with. But this does not often happen. Most children have a deep desire for a home and parents and will sense the adopters' acceptance and affection just as surely as they will know at once if adopters feel critical and rejecting. The love and warmth the new parents offer may enable the child to make the move more easily than one would expect. This was certainly true in the case of Terry.

Older children are usually deeply afraid that adoptive or foster parents will not like them and will send them back. They wonder what will happen if they wet the bed or break something. Sometimes they fear they cannot live up to new and higher standards of behaviour. Often these children believe that as soon as the adopters find out what they are really like, the bad parts as well as the good, they will no longer be loved or wanted. Their feelings about going to a new home are mixed. Often there have been other new homes which did not last. It is hard for them to believe this one is different and will last.

Some youngsters cover these fears with a pretended indifference and 'don't care' attitude. Some try desperately to win approval and love by model behaviour and a kind of false affection. Some are sullen and shy, others cheeky and loud. None of these attitudes is easy to live with and understand but these feelings are natural and almost inevitable in the situation and will pass as the child begins to feel secure.

## MEETINGS WITH NATURAL PARENTS

In recent years, it has become increasingly usual for natural and adoptive parents to have a brief meeting, usually just before the child is placed. It is most often the baby's birth mother who comes but occasionally his father or a grandparent may be present too.

Your first reaction may be surprise and a feeling that you would not want to do anything like that. Do not be too quick to refuse the opportunity. Most adoptive parents who have experienced such a meeting say that they were apprehensive and doubtful at first. Afterwards they were very glad indeed to be able to think of their child's birth mother as a real person and to have had the chance to find out a little more about her and her family. As one mother put it: 'Until then, I'd allowed myself to pretend that our baby would just appear from nowhere. As we talked to Janet, I realised that she could have been me ten years ago.'

The main purpose of these meetings is to give the mother the satisfaction of knowing that she is giving her child to people who truly want him and the reassurance of seeing them for herself. When you think about it, this does not seem a lot to ask does it? Most of us would want to do the same under the circumstances. Some mothers are too shy, others feel they will be looked down on or criticised and some feel a meeting would be too upsetting. But when they are given the chance, many do choose to meet.

It is not a question of wanting to 'give adopters the once-over to see if they will do'. Most mothers have already made their decision and trust their social worker to select a family. In fact it seems to be very rare for a mother to express any reservations about adopters she has met. What she wants is to be able to picture the people who will be bringing up her child. Some mothers want to give the child to them physically though more often the baby will not be present. The meetings are usually quite brief. They may be at a foster home or the agency office but will never be at your home. Introductions are by first name only and the social worker is there to help break the ice. If you already have children, it usually helps to bring them along.

While the original reason for arranging meetings was to help the natural parents, experience has shown that adopters get benefits too. It is reassuring to learn for yourself that the person who bore the child wants you to take over the role of parent. Perhaps more important is the way a meeting dispels fantasies. If one does not know much about someone it is easy to let your imagination run riot. Stephen's adoptive mother wrote about it like this:

> Until we met Dawn, I couldn't get out of my mind a newspaper story and picture of a woman who had battered her child to death. It was such a relief to discover what a nice girl Dawn is. I am so glad that in future years I shall be able to tell Stephen that we liked his mother so much. Dawn seemed to like us, too, so I hope this will be some help to her when she is feeling sad and lonely. Please give her our love when you next see her and tell her I haven't forgotten my promise to send a photograph of Stephen. We plan to have some proper ones taken soon and I will send you one to give to Dawn.

Natural mothers can be greatly helped by the personal and sympathetic interest of adoptive parents. Many of them need news and pictures of the baby at least during the early months when they are adjusting to their loss. Adoptive parents often agree to send a photograph at the time of legal adoption. Others start sending news much sooner and a few continue the correspondence considerably longer. The baby's first birthday is a time when mothers often greatly appreciate some news. Provided the agency acts as postman and go-between there need be no loss of confidentiality in these meetings and exchanges. Surnames and addresses will not be exchanged and identifying details can be avoided.

INTRODUCTORY VISITS

If you are adopting a young baby, you will very likely be able to take him home within a day or so of your first meeting. But if your new child is more than 6 months old, you will now be embarking on a period of introductory visits. You, or the child, or both may need more time before making a definite commitment and you will certainly need to get to know each other better and prepare yourselves for the reality of living together. If you are already parents, the introductory visits will provide the opportunity for your existing children and the newcomer to start getting acquainted.

The timing and style of these visits will depend on the child's age and on practical considerations like transport and distance. With older babies and toddlers, it is usually best for visits to start on the child's home ground so that he feels safe in familiar surroundings. You can gradually take him out on short trips and then to your house for a few hours or even overnight. Because a little child has no sense of time, your visits will need to be close together or he will forget you in between and there will be no build up of trust or friendliness.

If the distance is too great for easy visiting, you may want to consider finding somewhere to stay nearby for a few days of intensive contact before you take your child home for good. Some adopters have found it helpful to rent or borrow a caravan for this purpose.

Older children can tolerate slightly longer gaps between visits, but even with them, the meetings do need to be regular and quite frequent. Phone calls and postcards in between will help. Visiting can cause quite a lot of strain on new parents. Fetching and carrying a child to your home every week-end for several weeks can be tiring especially if the traffic is bad or you have to rely on public transport. The social worker may be able to help sometimes, but it will be up to you to do most of the travelling.

The number of introductory visits is likely to vary from three to six or more. Prospective adopters and social workers are quite apt to find themselves disagreeing about how long the visiting should go on. Maybe social workers tend to be too cautious and try to slow things down. Often, adoptive parents are in too much of a hurry. Because they feel sure themselves, they forget how much 'transition work' the child has to do. It is important to remember that at this stage the child has to look back as well as forward. There are doors to be closed as well as exciting new doors to open.

When the time comes for your new child to move in with you permanently, you will want to make sure that he tidies up the ends of his past life, says definite goodbyes to important people and places and brings his belongings with him. You do not want him to leave one foot in his old life or to feel that his birth parents or foster parents are expecting him back. Even if it should be decided that he 'stay for good' after a successful holiday with you, there needs to be a definite break and a return to the children's home or foster home for packing and farewells though these might be condensed into a very brief visit. It is not a good idea for a holiday placement or trial visit just to drift into something long-term.

It is a good idea to take all the opportunities you can to visit the children's home or foster home where your future child is living. This will give you a valuable opportunity to see what his world has been like. Just as one understands a fiancée better after visiting future parents-in-law, so it will help to learn as much as possible about your child's present way of life. Try to see for yourself how meals are served, what the bath and bedtime routines are, how much the children's activities are supervised and planned. Then you can begin to compare and consider these ways and those in your household.

A child who comes to you from a foster home will at least be used to family living even if there are many differences in life style. But if your child has spent a good many years in a children's home, a number of everyday things are likely to seem very strange to him and you will need to be aware and tactful about explanations.

Family budgets and institution budgets are differently planned. A child from a home is likely to be careless with clothes and equipment and very extravagant with hot water. He will probably see nothing wrong with running the washing machine to rinse through a few articles that could as well be done by hand. But he may never have been allowed to help himself to fruit or a snack in the way many family children would expect to do. At meal times a home child will probably expect an adult to serve out all the food and may not be at all used to helping himself from dishes on the table. He is not likely to see meals as a social occasion. In fact family meals may at first be quite a difficult experience for him and make him feel very much the outsider. In the early days, rather casual meals and very simple, ordinary food are likely to be best.

If you have ever been to stay with people you do not know very well, you will remember that one of the difficulties can be not having enough to do in a strange house. This can also be a problem for a youngster coming to visit especially if you do not already have children in the family. You will want to lay in a few inexpensive or second-hand games, books and comics including some things to do alone and some to do together. Err on the side of getting something too easy rather than complicated construction kits or games that require real skill. An insecure child will refuse to involve himself in something he fears he cannot achieve.

Since one purpose of the visit is to give the youngster a chance to see what living in your home would be like, you do not want to buy expensive presents or arrange too many special treats. On the other hand you will need some activities to enjoy together. These can be something very ordinary like washing the car, baking a cake, a trip to the supermarket or a local football game. Some things, of course, you will have to 'play by ear' as you see how the visit goes, but advance planning helps if you do not stick to it too rigidly.

The following suggestions may be of use:

1    The child will feel more comfortable if you show that a space has been made for him – at the table, in the toy cupboard and in the toothbrush rack.
2    Avoid competitive situations where the child may feel threatened and unable to cope.
3    Don't expect him to meet too many strange people all at once.
4    If you decide to involve your young relatives or neighbourhood children, think ahead to how you will introduce this visiting child and explain his presence with you. (See next chapter for suggestions about 'cover stories'.)

In many different ways you will need to be alert and sensitive to the child's readiness to commit himself to staying permanently. Tracy aged 10 longed for a pretty bedroom to herself, but when asked on her first visit to pick out curtain and wallpaper patterns for 'her' room, she felt pressured and retreated into an apparent indifference which was quite hurtful to her prospective parents. Another little girl might have revelled in this early demonstration of a wish to have her as a permanent member of the family. Each child has to move at his own pace and prospective parents and social workers have to pick up the clues on progress and time their moves accordingly.

Introductory visits are an essential step to a successful placement but it is well to remember that no one is behaving quite naturally. The child is a guest and you are hosts. This is not the relationship of parent and child. The youngster will probably be on his best behaviour and may not feel free to be his usual self.

There are sure to be some storms ahead and it is as idle for you to hope that the child will keep up this model conduct as for him to assume that you will always be so tolerant and ready to put yourself out to amuse and entertain him.

If he is homesick for the other children and familiar places, unenthusiastic about your activities and seems quite anxious to get back to the children's home or foster home, there is no need for despair. Though it may be disappointing and a blow to your hopes, it does not necessarily mean that the child does not like you or want to live with you. Usually it is just that he needs more time to get to know you. He needs to find out whether you really want him and if he can trust you to keep your word. If you promised to take him back on Sunday evening, will you do it? If you say you will come for him next week, will you be there? Many of these children have been let down by adults again and again.

### THE PRESENT CARETAKERS

You will probably need to exercise a lot of tact and sensitivity in your dealings with your child's present caretakers. It can be quite a difficult situation for both sides but, for the child's sake, the adults involved have got to achieve a smooth transition period. Remember that his caretakers probably know the child better than anyone and will have many pieces of information, memories and suggestions to share. These can make your parenting job easier and the child's move and adjustment less stressful.

The more the present caretakers have loved the child and the more effort they have put into helping him overcome his problems and get ready to join a new family, the more anxious they will be in case you are not, after all, the right parents for him. For your part, you may feel concerned and critical about some aspects of the care and training they have provided, or you may worry in case you cannot maintain the excellent standards they have achieved.

Most foster parents and residential staff are generous-minded people, deeply concerned about children's welfare and anxious to do everything they can to make this placement a success. Occasionally, however, a real problem can arise when a child's present caretakers are opposed to the adoption plan. The youngster will surely sense their feelings, even if they do not voice them, and may start to cling and say he does not want to move. An anxious or possessive houseparent or foster mother can, perhaps unintentionally, sabotage the whole placement especially if her feelings are not recognised.

It is the social worker's responsibility to prepare and support these adults through the move, but adopters can help by being thoughtful and considerate and by recognising how hard it can be to lose a child one has loved and cared for even if this has been part of one's job. Notes or phone calls to say how the child is settling down will be much appreciated.

# CHAPTER XV

# Bringing your child home

It is an unfortunate fact that many of us are much too inquisitive about our neighbours' affairs. Most people enjoy gossip. As this is so, and as adoption is still newsworthy, it is no good hoping that the arrival of a child for adoption will pass without comment or inquiries. Indeed, if your child is old enough to be out and about in the community, you will want to pave the way for him a bit. Without disclosing unsuitable personal details, you can, for instance, explain to close friends and neighbours that Johnny is coming to live with you, that you hope to adopt him and that he has previously been living in a children's home. If the youngster has any handicaps, prepare people for these with a simple explanation of the things he may not be able to do. The objective is to enlist their interest and support on your child's behalf as he adjusts to the new community. In the long run, of course, you will want your child to be accepted as a perfectly ordinary member of the group and it is to be hoped that, as time passes, the fact of his adoption will cease to be of general interest.

Experience has shown that it is best not to give people details of the child's background. The less your friends and relations know about the child's biological family the sooner they will feel that he is yours and the less likelihood there will be of neighbourhood gossip. There will not be so much to gossip about!

Memories are very unreliable. The simple facts you give when your child first comes may have been distorted beyond recognition a few years later. You can never be sure that some malicious or unthinking person may not damage your child by casual or unkind remarks or by information given in the wrong way. You might have told someone that Mary's mother had had a nervous breakdown, but it may come back to Mary that her father was criminally insane. Such things have happened. It can also be very hurtful to a child to discover that others know things about him that he does not know himself. Sometimes almost complete strangers can be incredibly nosy and rude, asking all kinds of detailed questions. Others are genuinely interested, but however difficult or embarrassing it may be, it really is much wiser to refuse to give specific answers. Once you start to tell things it is hard to stop.

Often the easiest thing to say is that the adoption agency has advised against giving this information to anyone at all and you feel their advice is good. Any suspicion that this means you are trying to hide something will be avoided if you always add that the child's history is quite satisfactory to you.

It is not only you adults who will be subject to questions. Carl and Helen Doss, who have adopted twelve children, write helpfully about this in their book *If You Adopt a Child*. They say:

> Your worst trial will be those who are unthinking enough to ask questions right in front of your child. Even a small toddler knows when he is being talked about and a seemingly preoccupied elementary school child will catch every word that is said in his hearing. Too many adults chatter thoughtlessly in front of children, as if they thought the small fry were stone deaf or non-existent.
>
> Sooner or later someone will point to your child and ask curiously, 'Where did you get him?' Your youngster may even be standing between the two of you, mouth agape and all ears for your answer. . . . Turn to your child with your arm around him, or wink him into the conversation with something like, 'Well, the Agency brought us together, and I guess it was just a matter of love at first sight.' Make it clear to your friends that if they are going to discuss your child in his presence, he can hear you – and he has feelings too!

The child himself should be helped to develop a strategy for dealing with awkward questions. He is almost certain to be asked things like 'Where did you come from?' 'Why don't you live with your own parents?' 'Are you adopted?' Kay Donley, a very experienced American adoption worker, has coined the expression 'cover story' for the strategy which every older child joining a new family needs to develop. The point is not that the child should be taught to conceal his past as though it were something shameful, but that he be helped to protect his personal private life from unfriendly or prying eyes. If he chooses to talk about his past with his close friends, that is an entirely different matter.

Without a 'cover story' many fostered and adopted children either give information which they afterwards regret disclosing or, more likely, they make up wild and fantastic tales and get a reputation for being untruthful. Handicapped youngsters may need to develop special skill in explaining their condition.

You will need to help your child to understand that every family has its private affairs which are not normally discussed with outsiders, that he does not have to give complete answers to casual questioners and that there are socially acceptable ways of getting out of awkward situations. The 'cover story' does not need to be complicated but it must make sense to the child and be acceptable to him. Finding out how he has been used to explaining himself is often a necessary first step. You can make up and play a game in which he is the questioner and you the child and then you reverse roles. Simple responses are usually enough, e.g. 'My first parents couldn't look after me any more.' 'This is my family now.' 'I used to live in Swindon (or Newcastle or Aberdeen).' 'Excuse me, but I have to go home to lunch now.' 'You would have to ask my family about that.'

## NAMES

The whole question of changing an adopted child's first name is worth some serious thought. It is very natural to want to give a baby a name that you have chosen and a young baby will not notice anything different. But discarding the name his first mother chose feels a bit like discarding his past and denying his origins. Increasingly, adopters are solving the dilemma by keeping the original name as a middle name so the child does not lose his original identity.

A child past infancy but too young to be consulted may find a change of name very confusing and upsetting. Just as he is beginning to understand himself as an individual person, he finds that he is apparently someone else! If there are reasons why changing a toddler's name seems absolutely necessary, you might use both old and new names together for a while and then quietly drop the old one.

For a school-age child both his first name and his surname will have great emotional significance. It will usually be out of the question to try and change an older child's first name. Every now and then a child will actually prefer a change. He may dislike his present name for some reason or it may have unhappy connections, but he will need to realise that a new name will not work a magic, remove the past or change everything about him. Many older children have chosen a new middle name at the time of adoption and may get great satisfaction from a name which ties them into their new family.

It is no longer unknown for an older child to retain his own surname even after legal adoption, but this is unusual and if adoption is definitely planned it will probably be best for the child to use your surname from the start. Most schools willingly agree to this when the situation is explained. If, however, the placement is for fostering with only a possibility of adoption, you will need to consult your social worker. In every case you will of course want to talk it over with the child. He may not be ready to give up his own name just yet. It is, after all, quite a lot to ask of him.

Then there is the question of what the new child is going to call you. He may have definite ideas about this himself. When Rosemary aged 6 was invited to call her new parents Ron and Helen, she quite indignantly replied that she would rather call them Mummy and Daddy. David had never known his father but was fond of his mother who was permanently in a mental hospital. He called his new father Dad from the very first day, but it was eight or nine months before he could bring himself to call his new mother Mum. Often a child will speak of his new parents as 'my mother and father' quite a long time before he can use these terms to their faces. It is all part of the difficult job of letting go of the past and accepting all the implications of a new way of life.

### ANNOUNCEMENTS AND VISITORS

Many people now put an announcement in the newspaper telling of the 'happy event' of adoption. It is wiser not to do this, however, until the legal formalities are complete. Although adoption is now much more open than it used to be, it is unwise for the two sets of parents to have each other's address. So do not give your address or the child's exact birth date in the announcement. If you say something like, 'To John and Mary Smith (née Brown) of Nottingham, a son Peter by adoption, now aged 8 months', all your close friends and relatives will know who you are. One advantage of a delay in making a general announcement is that it gives you time to get settled into your new routine before you have to start answering letters and seeing many visitors.

It is not good for a tiny baby to be picked up and handled by many strange people. With an older baby the picking up and fussing would not matter much if he had been with you since birth, but a newly-adopted baby has as much as he can do during the first few weeks to get used to a new mother and father and a few close friends and relatives. An older child will be equally ill at ease with strangers.

Naturally everyone will be looking forward to seeing the newcomer and you will be longing to show him off, but it might be best to say firmly before the great homecoming day that you will not be having friends in for a while. In your first enthusiasm on hearing the news it is easy to make rash invitations which you afterwards regret.

No one expects a mother just home from the hospital to give a party. It is true that you have not had the physical effort of childbirth, but adoption involves considerable emotional strain and you, too, have to get used to new routines, extra work and all the adjustments involved in becoming a larger family. You also have to endure the small, gnawing fear that it is just possible that something might occur to delay or prevent the adoption. Your child is still not legally yours. It will not be at all surprising if you are often tired and sometimes irritable.

Although you do not want a lot of adult visitors, you will want to give an older child opportunities to make friends in the locality. It is not always a good idea to move a child into a new family at the beginning of a long school holiday. The time is apt to hang heavy on his hands if he has not had a chance to make school friends, and child and new parents do not get much chance for the very necessary 'breathers' from each other's company. Learning to live as a family is hard work and everyone will need an occasional respite.

## JOYS AND SORROWS OF THE FIRST FEW MONTHS

The wonderful day when you take your child home brings the fulfilment of your deep desires. This is the moment you have looked forward to for so long. For your new child it is different. You have only gained, but he has also lost something. He may be so little that the loss of his birth mother and the change of home is felt only vaguely. But we can be sure that the child does notice the difference and probably has a sense of loss, particularly if he has been breast-fed for a time and then abruptly weaned.

If your baby is over 3 or 4 months and has learned to distinguish faces and places, he is going to need your help and sensitive understanding while he gets used to his new surroundings and learns to love you. The older he is the more help he will need and the longer it may take him to feel really at home.

The very special problems which arise in the early months of older child adoptions need a chapter to themselves, so for the moment, let's just consider babies and toddlers who are joining new families.

We do not know exactly how a tiny baby feels about things, but we do know that he feels strongly not just with his emotions, but with his whole body, his circulation and his digestion. The newborn baby is 'all one piece'. He knows only general comfort and discomfort. If he is hungry he hurts all over. All his needs are intimately bound up with one another. Sucking, for instance, is necessary for a baby, not only to eat but to help circulation, breathing, and to relax tension. It is also a baby's first intimate contact with another person and the outside world.

Anyone who wants to gain a deeper understanding of a baby's physical and emotional needs should read Margaret Ribble's book *The Rights of Infants*. Dr Ribble has much to say that will be valuable for adoptive parents. Among other things she stresses the infant's reaction to change. She writes,

> The extreme sensitivity of the infant to such factors as changes in temperature, light or sound, handling by strange persons, slight differences in ventilation or in hardness or softness of the bed, is not usually appreciated. It is difficult for an adult to realise how extremely distressing it is to the young infant to have to become adjusted to the new world. One is reminded of seedlings that wilt on transplanting and must be specially tended and protected. We find, for example, that when a baby is placed in a room where sudden loud noises occur, such as from a street car passing at frequent intervals, a doorbell ringing or a sudden clatter of dishes, he reacts sharply to the sudden stimulation. On the other hand, our study showed that when infants were taken home from a hospital nursery where there was more or less a bustle of human sounds and where lights went on and off, they gave an equally strong reaction to the stillness of an entirely quiet room. As we have said, the stimulation given a small baby has to be as carefully regulated as his food intake if the child is to be nervously stable.

This will give adopters some clues on how to spare a baby unnecessary upsets. Detailed inquiries about his previous routine and thoughtful planning of his new life can do much to help. Careful observation of his reactions and a sensitive catering to his needs will help even more.

If for a moment we try to put ourselves into the very small shoes of a child between 6 months and 3 years old, we find that the world seems very large, strange and often frightening. Familiar people, things and places provide the only real security; feelings are intense and fears are vivid but cannot be expressed in words. We shall soon realise that change of any sort is alarming.

The very young child can only venture out from a secure base. When he first arrives in a new place he will cling to any familiar object. It is important to try to arrange for an adopted child to bring some of his clothes and well-loved toys with him to ease the strangeness. Some children have a speical toy or object which is essential to their happiness. Terry, who was mentioned in a previous chapter, had a little blue blanket to which he was devoted. He clung to it in moments of stress and often carried it about with him. When he first went to the Hursts' home his dependence on the blanket increased very much. He kept it with him night and day, including meal-times. When it got too dirty to be endured, Joan Hurst cut it in two so that Terry could keep one half while she washed the other! As he became secure he needed it less and less, until finally he left it on his cot all day, needing its comforting presence only when he was falling asleep.

The more details you have about the youngster's usual routine the easier it will be to help him during the first difficult days. Of course his old routine may not suit your household, and you can change it gradually later, but at first he will feel happier with the same foods, sleep periods and toys that he had before. Having the same routines will also help him realise that you, too, know how to look after him.

If the child is old enough to talk it will help him to talk about his previous life and the people he knew. It will be easier for you to do this if you know the names he used for important people in his past. Accept whatever he tells you without surprise or dismay and do not worry if you know some of the things he says are pure fantasy or wishful thinking. He may tell you that his other daddy had two private aeroplanes or that his foster mother put the kitten through the mincer. He is not really telling lies. He is telling you about a world of imagination which is very real to him and trying to make sense of his past and the strange, uncomfortable things that have happened to him. If he does not bring up the subject himself, it is best not to poke and pry because it may not be the right time for him, but make some opportunities for him to talk and show a friendly but casual interest.

A very useful piece of equipment in any adoptive family is an old fashioned rocking chair. It will be particularly helpful if your new child is a pre-schooler. Being rocked on someone's lap is soothing to a troubled child. It enables him to feel like a baby again if he wants to. Adult and child can rock together companionably without talking, but it may also be easy to talk because in a rocking chair one is not 'face to face'. For the same reason, children sometimes talk very confidentially when riding in a car.

The key words for those adopting toddlers are patience and flexibility. Because of his past experiences, it may be many months before your adopted child feels really settled and secure. He may not immediately measure up to the standards of the more fortunate children of your friends and relatives. Given love and patience he probably will catch up, and perhaps surpass them, but this takes time.

Does it really matter if your youngster has to wear nappies a little longer than the boy next door, if his table manners are poor at first or his speech is less distinct? It may be tiresome, but does it really matter? As he begins to love you he will want to please you and learn your ways of doing things. If you immediately start an intensive improvement campaign which requires nagging reminders, scoldings and fussing, it will be difficult for him to learn to love you. The basis of good manners is liking people and wishing to make them comfortable. If you can help your child to like and trust people, the manners will come of their own accord.

Some families have at first been delighted with their new child's independence, clean habits, conformity to bed and bath times, and other signs of early training. They are dismayed when after a few weeks all these good habits seem to vanish; the child wets, soils, clings to the mother, has temper tantrums and generally seems to go back to much more babyish behaviour. This is bound to be rather disconcerting, but may in truth be a very good sign for your child's future emotional health. He may need the experience of being your baby.

There is no need to be afraid that if you treat him as a baby for a while he will stay that way. Those unattractive and irresponsible adults, who seem childish and selfish, have almost certainly become so from too little real mothering, not too much. They are still searching for a fundamental experience which they have never had. Provided you watch carefully for signs of independence, and encourage your child to develop his initiative, self-reliance and self-control just as soon as he feels able, you need not fear that you will make him dependent. Independence cannot be successfully imposed on a person who is not ready for it. That is like expecting a jelly to set before it has had time to cool.

People used to think that a child who had had a close attachment to his mother or a foster mother would not be able to take on a new family. But this is not so. Given understanding, explanations, time and loving acceptance, such a child can come to love new parents. We do not have to stop loving one person because we start loving another. Because a child keeps a loving memory of his first mother or foster mother, it does not mean that he cannot love you too.

In fact, if the child you take into your home sorrows over the people he has left behind, you should be truly thankful. It may be rather disappointing if you are not able to make him entirely happy immediately, but it is a sign that you have a child with the precious capacity to love deeply. In a little while he will have the same long-lasting love for you.

Perhaps it will help to consider the child as a plant and love as the flower. Some flowers, like the Scarlet Pimpernel, close up in cold or wet weather. In the same way the stress and strain and strangeness of the move may temporarily close your child's ability to show his love. With warmth and security the flower will open again.

It could be that your plant has been stunted by a harsh environment and though the leaves and stem have developed there is no sign of a flower. Just so, some children who have been institutionalised or pushed from pillar to post have never developed the flower of love. Their bodies and minds have grown but their emotions are still stunted and frozen.

Adoptive parents who are doing the enormously important job of restoring and developing a child's power to love need the patience and knowledge of a gardener raising a delicate but valuable flower. They too must surround the child with all the conditions necessary for healthy growth – the warmth of their love offered but not forced, the nourishment of an understanding home and the support of wise guidance and control. The gardener may have to wait several seasons before his flower blossoms, and adoptive parents cannot expect quick results. They will have to give and give without stint, but their reward and satisfaction will be very great.

While we are on the subject of love, it may be as well to consider for a moment the very real possibility that at first one or both of you will not love this little newcomer as deeply as you expected. This can cause adopters much distress but need not be a cause for alarm and anxiety. Many mothers report that it was weeks or even months before they really loved babies they had given birth to and just the same thing can happen to adoptive parents. Love takes its own time to grow, sometimes very fast and sometimes more slowly.

It is also well to be aware of the adjustments which new parents have to make in their relationship to one another. For instance, husbands may have to get used to a change if they have previously been the centre of attention when they get home from work. Even in the best-organised households there will be times when the baby cries and cries, meals are late or the ironing not done. Wives now have to show pleasure in toy cars, dolls and trains instead of gifts of chocolates and roses. It is all too easy to let a little jealousy slip in to mar the happiness. If either partner has been an only child, used to being the centre of attention, it may be quite hard to learn to share wife or husband with a baby. There is no need to be ashamed of these fleeting feelings, so long as they are recognised and checked with a dash of common sense.

It is good to remember that love is not limited. The more we love the more we can love. A wife does not love her husband less because she seems so taken up with the baby and is sometimes tired out by the end of the day. She probably loves him more as they share together the experience of being parents. A husband does not stop loving and admiring his wife because he keeps remarking on his baby daughter's blue eyes or pretty curls. It may be a little tactless of him to forget to pay his wife compliments too, but it does not mean lack of affection.

# CHAPTER XVI

# Trials and traumas in older child placements

'I think we must warn them that they may be tested to the limit', said Eileen.

'And it's no good expecting too much of the child too soon,' said Susan, 'I think we ought to emphasise that.'

'But we want to explain the good side of it, too', chipped in Vivienne, and she sat back in her chair with a quiet little smile as though remembering something pleasant.

Eileen, Susan and Vivienne were sitting round a table in social worker George Finney's office drinking coffee and planning a series of discussion groups for prospective adopters. George had asked them to come and share their experiences of adopting an older child. He felt that the most satisfactory way to learn is to talk to someone who has done it and that these three adoptive mothers all had something special to offer. George wanted those attending the groups to realise that in spite of everyone's best efforts, not every adoption placement is going to work out. But nine out of ten do succeed and the ultimate joy and satisfaction of parents and children make the hard work, risks and heartaches seem worth while.

George had invited Eileen because after successfully adopting Charlene at age 11, she and her husband had applied to adopt Derek aged 8 and he had joined their family five weeks ago. After a deceptively calm 'honeymoon' period, Derek was now trying out and testing for all he was worth. Since his short life had given him no reason to trust anyone, his testing was likely to be very thorough.

'There are days', said Eileen, 'when I wonder how much more we can take. We had the same pattern with Charlene of a very easy first few weeks and then a very difficult patch, but she never carried it as far as Derek does and she tended to be withdrawn and too quiet rather than badly behaved.'

'Do you think that having Charlene is a help?' asked George, 'or does it make things more complicated?' 'I find it a real help', replied Eileen. 'Charlene is very patient with Derek. I think she knows how he feels.' 'Seeing her reassures me that I must be a reasonable parent even on days when I feel I'm making no progress with Derek. But I'm sounding gloomier than I feel,' she added. 'I don't want to put people off adopting. Derek's a marvellous kid underneath all the aggro and I don't regret our decision to take him except at the odd moment when I'm really, really tired.'

Vivienne and Susan wanted to know more about Derek's behaviour and Eileen explained that he was tense and up-tight and had terrible temper tantrums when he kicked and broke things. 'He wets the bed most nights,' she said, 'and he has an insatiable appetite for chocolate and cake. He pinches Charlene's sweets and I'm worried that he may start stealing from our local shop if I try to cut down on his sweet eating at home.'

Susan, the oldest and most experienced of the three mothers, recalled that her adopted son James had the same craving for sweet things when he came to them at age 12 having spent his early years in a rather bleak boys' home. 'James didn't steal, but he hoarded food under his pillow', she said. 'It used to make a horrible mess.'

Vivienne sympathised with Eileen over the wet beds having had the same problem with her Joyce who had wet her bed nightly until the day of the adoption hearing when it stopped almost completely. 'That was over a year after we had her', Vivienne explained. 'I think that until the judge told her there was no way anyone could take her from us, she hadn't been able to believe she was safe and that Henry and I were truly Mum and Dad for always. Even now', Vivienne went on, 'we get the occasional wet bed if Joyce is upset about something although she's 10 years old now and terribly ashamed about it.'

'I've come to the conclusion', said Susan, 'that we all tend to underestimate the difficulties these kids have in adjusting to a new family. Now that James is nearly grown up, we can all sit and talk about his early life and the time he came to us. I've been shocked to realise how little I appreciated what he was going through and how frightened he was that we wouldn't want him. He had such a low opinion of himself that it took me several weeks to persuade him that he ought to use a capital letter when he wrote the word I. He didn't think he was important enough to merit a capital. He lied all the time, too, either to make himself feel big or because he was too scared to own up to anything even if we asked a simple question like "Who's taken the hammer out of the tool chest?" He cheated at games as well. We used to get furious with him because our own children had never done that sort of thing. Looking back, I think we made things worse because we tried to tackle the symptoms instead of trying to understand why he behaved like that. At one point my husband even thought James must be basically dishonest. We just didn't appreciate what was going on.'

'I think I knew what was going on with Joyce', said Vivienne, 'because she made it so clear that she wanted desperately to stay with us. My trouble was that I didn't really love Joyce for ages. I felt terrible when the poor child was trying so hard to please and yet sometimes she aggravated me so that I felt like screaming. She was forever clinging and kissing and it just didn't feel genuine. I realise now that she'd just never had enough affection and people kept coming and going in and out of her life. Since she knows she belongs she's changed a lot and when she gives me a hug now I know she means it.'

George wondered when Vivienne's feelings towards Joyce had changed and what caused it to happen. 'Well,' she said, 'it wasn't anything dramatic. The first Easter we had her my mother came to the rescue and had Joyce for a week so that Henry and I could go to Malta for a week's holiday. I'd had 'flu and Joyce was really getting me down. I was at the point of telling the social worker that she'd have to find her another family. But somehow, when we got home again I was really glad to see Joyce, and she gave us such a big welcome. It was a lovely feeling. After that things gradually got better until one day Joyce was very late home from school and I was worried sick about her. I realised then that I did care about her a lot and she had become truly part of the family without my noticing it.'

TESTING IS A GOOD SIGN

As Eileen, Susan and Vivienne talked and reminisced and planned with George Finney how best to present their experiences to the group, they gradually decided that they would concentrate on the fact that every child going into a new home has to test it out to make sure that it is safe and will last. 'Somehow', said George, 'we have got to help people to see that testing is a good sign.'

Just as a body runs a temperature to combat an infection and get back to health, so a deprived child mobilises his strength to deal with loss, change and stress. He is fighting for emotional survival and he has to find out where he stands. Can you love him as he really is, 'warts and all'? Will you get tired of him after a while and send him back? How far can you really be trusted? Do you mean what you say or make empty promises? These are the urgent but unspoken questions that lie beneath the demanding, aggressive or withdrawn behaviour of the newly-placed child.

When you are on the receiving end of the testing it is very hard to keep remembering this. You will wonder why, if he wants to belong, your new child should apparently be doing everything in his power to make himself so unbearable that no family on earth would want to keep him. Often the bad behaviour is particularly hard to take because it follows an early 'honeymoon' when everything went remarkably smoothly. You know the youngster can make himself agreeable, and you begin to wonder whether you are doing something wrong and provoking this unwelcome response. To find the answer to the riddle, look behind the behaviour to the reason for it. The over-riding reason is fear.

Every older child joining a new family feels that he has been rejected by his own people and by others along the way. It makes no difference whether his first parents could help it or not – even death *feels* like desertion to a child. Because he feels rejected, he feels unlovable and very, very insecure.

Although he fears he is unlovable he wants to be loved. It is a basic part of human nature that we all want to be special to someone who will love us unconditionally. Underneath every defiant, demanding, apparently insolent or uncaring youngster is a small boy or girl longing to be appreciated and wanted. Every parentless child desperately wants to be 'ordinary', to have a mum and dad and a normal home.

Nothing is so hard to bear as uncertainty. 'Tell me the worst' we say when we fear bad news. It is better to know than live in doubt. If one is going to be rejected again, it is better to get it over with. The newly-placed child cannot believe you mean it when you say this can be his home 'for always'. He has to find out if you will love and want him when he is bad and he has to show you how bad he can be and test you out. So *testing is a sign that he wants to belong*.

SOME PROBLEMS TO EXPECT AND WAYS OF COPING

Children react to stress in different ways according to their
temperament and life experiences. In some, the fear leads to
anger and aggression. Others withdraw into themselves, day-
dream, suck their thumbs, whine and cling, or seem totally disin-
terested and aloof. However, there are certain reactions which
are so usual that every adoptive or foster parent should be
prepared for them although, of course, not every child will
show every symptom.

*Bedwetting*

Bedwetting is so common a problem among troubled children
that you will be wise to invest in a plastic mattress cover whether
or not you have been warned that your future child wets his bed.
Occasionally there is a medical cause for bedwetting but it is
nearly always caused by some stress or tension over which the
child has no control. He really cannot help it.

Punishment is useless and unkind. Show confidence that of
course he will grow out of this later, as indeed he will, and give
plenty of praise for dry nights. Later on, if the wetting persists
and if, but only if, you have his genuine co-operation, it may be
worth asking your doctor about using one of the mechanical aids
like the bell and pad.

*No interests*

Some new parents find that one of the most exasperating and
perplexing problems is a child who has no interests and who sits
about all day watching TV or lounging around. There are various
reasons for this and understanding them can help you find ways
of improving the situation.

The first and probably most usual reason is that not only has
the child never been exposed to interesting hobbies or creative
activities, but he has never learned to play. This can happen to
youngsters in very disorganised families, to those brought up in
large groups or those who have moved many times to a variety of
environments. Such children literally have to be taught how to
play and have fun. You will have to involve yourselves actively in
games of all sorts and show him how to do and make things.
Make games out of chores and things you do together. At first
you may have to pitch the level to what one would normally
expect of a somewhat younger child.

Another common reason is that the child's low self-esteem and fear of failure make him unwilling to try anything new or enter into any competitive situation. He would rather be bored than risk not being able to do it right. In time you will be able to help a lot with this problem because you can gradually build up his self-confidence. Be sure to praise effort rather than achievement. Break down any new task into small, easy steps that he can master one by one. Introduce new activities carefully so that he can get the satisfaction of some success early on. Be very careful not to pour cold water on any ideas or interests but do not rush him into a new hobby or he may back off in fright.

Martha Dickerson is a foster parent who has written helpfully about her experiences. Martha and her husband cared for severely mentally handicapped boys but many of her ideas are useful for dealing with any deprived or troubled child. When discussing teaching cooking to a child with a short attention span she says:

> I found I could hold a boy's interest in the task by allowing him to be involved in those steps which were closest to the finished product. Andrew and I made a casserole together involving cooked rice, cream of mushroom soup, cashew nuts, chicken and black olives. It worked well for Andrew to open all the cans and stir everything together in the casserole. I do not believe he would have been interested in the process if he had had to stay in the kitchen while the rice cooked for 45 minutes. After he was able to see and eat his finished product, he would stay with the process for the entire time.

*Greed, stealing and hoarding*
Many deprived children are greedy and materialistic. Because they have been denied lasting love and satisfying personal relationships they set great store by things. Clothes, cars, gadgets of all kinds are important to them and they can be very demanding of gifts. Sharing and generosity are virtues based on feelings of security and trust. The insecure child cannot share because he needs everything to survive and cannot trust that there will be more tomorrow. Sweets seem to be a substitute for love and food is very, very important to newly-placed children. Many gorge themselves for a while but this phase usually passes quite soon. In the next phase, the same child may become very fussy and faddy. A youngster who has had too many changes and not enough love, attention and security may try to satisfy his inner longing by

hoarding food or small items. Many of these children also steal.

If your adopted child takes money from your purse or steals sweets or small things from the local shops, do not panic or think you have a confirmed thief on your hands. You have not. This sort of stealing is symbolic and not really a moral issue. Nevertheless you cannot ignore it; the child must not be allowed to think stealing does not matter. In the long run, the cure is to make him feel loved, wanted and secure. In the short run, make him refund anything he takes, try and keep him out of temptation and keep a close eye that he is not bringing home things that do not belong to him or buying unaccountably large quantities of sweets. If you are pretty sure he has stolen something, charge him with it but do not ask him if he did it because he will almost certainly lie to protect himself and thus be in worse trouble.

*Inability to express feelings appropriately*
Like Vivienne's adopted daughter Joyce, your child may tend to be indiscriminately and inappropriately affectionate, giving strangers the same hugs and kisses that he gives to the family. Or he may be at the other extreme and find it hard to show any affection at all, disguising his true feelings with an off-hand manner and finding it almost impossible to ask for help or comfort even if he is hurt.

Paul was 9 when he finally found a permanent home. He longed to be cuddled but could not let himself show it. So he invented a game in which he would jump from his bed into his parents' arms over and over again. Luckily, they realised that this gave the opportunity for hugs all round and so they encouraged the game in spite of the risk to the bed springs from Paul's energetic jumps.

Youngsters who have been sexually abused, either by adults or by older children, may not know how to approach people except by being seductive. This calls for re-education, not shock. By personal example and by direct teaching, the parent of the same sex as the child needs to demonstrate how to relate to others in a more suitable way.

Learning to deal with anger is another major area of difficulty. We all know that being frightened tends to make us angry. One's reaction to a child who darts into the road is to be furious and shake him. Since most youngsters placed for adoption are full of fears, they often feel angry and this feeling, too, is frightening because they do not know what to do with it.

In some, the tension explodes into temper tantrums – screaming, kicking and throwing things. Others cannot show their feelings so openly and resort to the much more subtle method of provoking other people to get angry instead. It is not always easy to recognise what is going on. The child who is careless and forgetful, the child who dawdles and messes with his food, is teasing his mother to lose her temper and at the same time testing her to see if she will produce the punishing, rejecting responses he feels he deserves.

Both sorts of children need help to recognise their angry feelings and let them out in acceptable ways. The child in the tantrum needs to be told: 'Don't scream, use words, then I can help.' The dawdling, teasing child may be helped by hearing you say: 'I think you must be feeling angry because . . .' or 'I think you are trying to make me angry with you.' Then you can suggest some ways of letting off steam. 'I can see you are feeling angry. Why don't you go and kick the football/stamp about a bit/get your play dough and bang it with the rolling pin/see how loud you can sing John Brown's Body.'

You can use the quiet time after a tantrum to get close. This is not the moment for punishment and, after all, no one thinks that husband and wife should not kiss and make up after a row.

*Lack of vocabulary*

The speech problems of many children in care are not just poor pronunciation, inaccurate grammar and over-use of swear words or vulgar expressions, though all these are usually present. An even more basic problem is that often these youngsters just do not know the words for things, feelings or ideas. In their first families there may have been little conversation between parents and children and vocabulary may have been limited. In group homes children talk to each other more than to adults and have little chance to listen to adult discussions. The lack of an adequate vocabulary may be accentuated if children are placed in middle-class adoptive homes where verbal skills are taken for granted.

The child with a very restricted vocabulary faces various difficulties.

1  He may literally not understand what is being said to him. In a family discussion he feels odd man out and he may develop all sorts of misconceptions about what is going on.

2  His new parents find it hard to grasp what he wants or feels because he expresses himself so inadequately. This makes

both child and adult upset and angry and leads to mis-
understandings and cross purposes.

3   At school he cannot understand written or verbal instructions and so produces poorer work, thus re-inforcing his
poor concept of his own ability.

Fortunately there are some fairly obvious ways of helping to
overcome language problems. In the beginning parents may
need to make a special effort to speak simply and in concrete
terms. They can also take steps to teach the child the names of
things; you may be startled to discover that your child does not
know the names of everyday household objects. He may not
know how to answer the telephone. Talking directly to the child
and encouraging him to reply by showing a real interest in what
he has to say is the best form of teaching. Playing singing games
and repeating rhymes and riddles is fun and can be done in odd
moments. Reading aloud is also excellent but it may be a while
before your child can relax enough to sit still and enjoy this.
Maybe you can lead into it through short bed-time stories or by
reading to him while he paints or makes a model.

*School problems*
No matter how intelligent they are, virtually all children joining
new families are behind with their school work. Just occasionally
it may be important to put early emphasis on helping your child
to achieve better, for instance by learning to read if this is a
problem, or by having extra help to catch up with subjects missed
by changes of school. Much, much more often, however, it is
better not to expect much improvement in school work until he
feels more secure in your home. He will probably have to invest
such a lot of emotional energy in coping with new relationships
that he will have little energy left for intellectual learning.

What is likely to create a more urgent problem is his behaviour
in the classroom. You will have to lay the groundwork carefully
in advance by discussion with the headmaster before your child
joins the school and then you should seek to make an ally of his
teacher and try never to let yourself get into conflict with her.
You must sympathise with her difficulty in coping with the
aggressive, attention seeking or withdrawn behaviour that your
child is likely to show, just as you want her to be sympathetic to
the strain he is under. You do not want her to think of him as a
'poor deprived waif' from whom nothing much can be expected,
but it will not help if he is asked to achieve something quite

beyond his present level of attainment. Above all he needs the satisfaction of succeeding because this will give him courage to risk trying harder.

### EXTRA PARENTING SKILLS CAN BE LEARNED

Even if you already have a good deal of experience of children, you will probably need to acquire some extra knowledge and parenting skills to cope with the problems your new child brings with him into your home. His behaviour will often be puzzling as well as provoking and your own reactions may surprise and displease you as well.

Many deprived children develop inappropriate ways of responding and have to be helped to unlearn them. They also transfer on to their new parents feelings which they have had about people in the past. Your new child will expect you to behave like the people he has been used to. If you are not careful, you could find yourself fulfilling these expectations and behaving quite unlike your usual self. Candace Wheeler, who is a very experienced American adoption worker, puts it like this:

> One of the things that happens when we are treated as if we were something we are not is that we begin to act the way the other person expects us to. Perhaps you can recall when a teacher was convinced that you were a capable student (or a dumb one), and you tried your hardest to live up to that good opinion (or down to that bad one). This is something called a 'self-fulfilling prophecy', which means that you make something happen by believing that it's going to happen. At times our children create self-fulfilling prophecies of their adoptive parents. By acting as if he expects mum and dad to fight about him, a child might unconsciously manoeuvre you into playing that role or acting as he expects. He has learned that's how life is, and he sets up situations to create the same results.
>
> Many older adoptive children have an uncanny ability to set parents up to reject them, and often neither parents or children realize what is happening until it is too late. So you need to try to look at your reactions and refuse to be 'typecast'. Your child needs to learn that his home is different; these parents don't play those old games. As he begins to have that assurance, he can begin to see you clearly for who you are, and not as repetitions of past experiences.

Just as you need to be more than usually aware of your reactions to the child and the way in which he is getting you to respond, so you need to keep an eye on what is going on in your marriage. Trying to absorb an older child into the family can create unexpected strains. You will want to be sure that you keep your channels of communication open and that you do not let the child side with one against the other. Do not give so much time, energy and attention to the child that you have none at all left for each other. You must get your own batteries re-charged now and then if you are to keep going effectively. Some time out together is a necessity, not a luxury.

Quite a lot of deprived children are experts at making one member of the family feel odd man out. They are good at this because they have experienced it themselves. When Paula and Mike Ricketts took Sarah into their home, Sarah and Mike got on very well from the start. When alone with her new mother, however, Sarah was very different – cheeky, defiant and often downright unpleasant. Mike secretly thought Paula was exaggerating until one day he came home from work early and heard for himself what was going on in the kitchen. As soon as Mike re-established his relationship with his wife, her problems with Sarah began to get better.

Quite a lot of children in care have been brought up almost exclusively by women. When they at last acquire a father they may ignore or fear him or they may focus all their attention and affection on him regarding the new mother merely as the provider of food and clean clothes. Colin aged 5 copied his new dad in every particular even insisting on wearing a tie with his T-shirt!

An essential tool to develop is what some would call the art of compromise and others the skill of arbitration. This does not mean giving in because a child whines, sulks or shouts. It means finding mutually acceptable solutions and avoiding confrontations as much as possible. If you feel a battle is essential, pick your ground carefully. You want to be sure you can win and just as you cannot make a baby go to sleep or use the pot, so there are situations in which you cannot make an older child obey you.

Children need limits and controls and it is no kindness to your child to let him go on being obnoxious or to treat him as a poor thing who cannot do any better. You must set standards even though some bad habits may have to be ignored for a time while you concentrate on more pressing problems. You may need to be quite strict and even punish at times, but a swift intervention to stop trouble before it gets going is the best possible method and praise nearly always works better than punishment. Giving adequate praise really is important. You do not want to despise rewards either. They work, especially if you praise and reward effort rather than achievement. There is no need to equate rewards with bribery. Bribery is a way of persuading someone to do something he should not do. Rewards are like prizes at school or bonuses at work. They are in recognition of extra effort.

To begin with at least, rewards need to be immediate. For instance, if you want to help a child stop biting his nails you can reward for each nail unbitten at the end of the week rather than wait until he can stop biting altogether. If the task is too difficult or the reward too long in coming, he will be discouraged and give up.

Rewards can be used effectively to encourage new skills. John and Helen Krumboltz have written a book called *Changing Children's Behaviour* in which they tell the story of Madeline who could read competently but seldom opened a book at home. Her father wanted her to learn the pleasures of reading. He offered a financial reward if she would choose a book from the library and read it within a week. He asked her what she thought this task was worth and Madeline, to whom the idea of reading a whole book looked very hard, said £3. This was a good deal more than her father had expected but he agreed. Madeline not only read the book in less than a week, she thoroughly enjoyed it. A little while later she asked her father what he would give her to read a second book. This time they settled on £1.50. Very soon Madeline was reading for pleasure and rewards were unnecessary.

Of course rewards will not usually be money. Praise, treats, gold stars and little extras are usually more suitable and rewards should only be large enough to achieve the aim of reinforcing good behaviour and encouraging effort. They should also be used thoughtfully. You need to study your child's behaviour and devise a strategy to deal with it. Often it helps to keep some notes of how and when things go wrong. By looking at a series of situations when your child got upset or misbehaved, you may be able to figure out what it is that makes him feel insecure and inadequate so that he responds inappropriately. Analysing your own behaviour and reactions is also useful.

Do not be too discouraged if you quite often feel that you did not handle a situation as well as you would have liked or if you sometimes 'lose your cool' and get really angry and upset. There is only one thing which you must never do and that is *threaten* to send him back. It will only make his insecurity ten times worse and though it might achieve a temporary improvement, in the long run it can only be a setback. The possibility that this adoption just will not work may have to be faced, but if you have to tell the child that he must leave, you do not want to do it when you are angry with him and it will nearly always be best to talk it over with your social worker first.

When you are making decisions about how to handle either big or little problems, it helps if you use your imagination and put yourself in the child's place. When you do this it is not difficult to realise how he may feel about certain things. For instance, if you criticise his first parents or his past caretakers it will feel as if you are belittling him too. He may make unfavourable comments about the children's home he was living in, but it will be most unwise for you to do so. Asking him to change his manners, his speech or his personal habits implies that his present ways are not good enough. Improvement in these things will almost certainly be necessary, but you need to go carefully about changing them and be aware of how he may react. Be sensitive too, towards his feelings for the clothes and possessions he brought with him. Some children will want to replace these as soon as possible, but most will cling to some battered or tattered items just as we all have a sentimental attachment to mementos from the past. Let him wear his familiar garments until he feels comfortable about switching to new ones.

It is usually best to start by identifying your child's good points and build on these rather than noting all the problem areas and setting out to cure them. In any case, a lot of his more aggravating habits will probably stop of their own accord if you can avoid making an issue of them. Children pick up the style and manners of those they live with and as he adapts to your home your child will gradually take on your ways, your speech and your outlook on life.

Try to avoid putting him into situations when he feels unsure about what is expected or does not know how to handle himself. Do not spring things on him or subject him to sudden changes if you can help it. Some very ordinary social occasions may be quite strange to him and because he is scared he may act stupid or boisterous or retire into a shell. You can help by discussing in advance just what will happen, who will be there and what his part in the affair will be. If possible, give him something definite to do like handing round the sandwiches. You may even need to make a game out of it and play at going out to tea with Great

Aunt Mabel or what happens on a train journey or how to go to the library and exchange a book. Remind yourself often that his social experiences may be very limited indeed.

Communication between parents and children is a big subject which can only be touched on here, but you and your new child will have to learn to read each other's signals. When you are with someone you know very well, marriage partner, parent, child or close friend, you often know how they are feeling or what they want without any exchange of words. You just know by their expression and gestures. To begin with, you and your new child cannot hope to have this sort of mutual understanding, but before long you will start to be able to de-code his messages.

It may take the child a good deal longer to appreciate how you feel. Although some deprived children are acutely aware of other people's feelings, some are too busy trying to cope with their own emotions to have any real interest in anyone else's feelings. Some cannot even identify their own feelings let alone anyone else's. This means that you need to make special efforts to ensure that your messages get through to him and do not just assume he will be aware of how you feel. Tell him in words, loud and clear how you are feeling and reacting. When you are angry, say so and explain why. When you are pleased or tired, disappointed or happy, let him know. As well as helping him to understand you, this will also set him an example of how to communicate his feelings to others.

Remember, too, that the words you use need to be simple and any instructions you give very full and clear. A newcomer to the family may genuinely not understand what you want done. Not wishing to look foolish by asking for explanations, he may well go off and do it wrong and this can easily look like deliberate naughtiness, or carelessness. So, don't just say: 'Get ready for lunch' but 'wash your hands, brush your hair and put away those painting things, lunch will be ready in five minutes.'

Another important skill that adoptive parents need to develop is knowing when to ask for help and where best to get it. This will, of course, be of obvious importance if your child has physical or mental handicaps. The various associations set up to help with particular problems can provide essential information and advice on the best ways to encourage the development of skills and promote acceptable behaviour. But even if your youngster is not officially handicapped, he is almost certain to have some emotional problems. These almost certainly have their roots far back in his past, long before you came into his life. There is no need to feel badly because you cannot untangle all the snarls or heal all the wounds without outside help. Just as you would seek the help of doctor or hospital for a physical illness, so you may need the expert advice of a psychiatrist or psychologist in addition to the help of your social worker.

Some adopters are tempted to cover up problems when the social worker visits and claim that everything is going smoothly even when it is not. If you expressed a lot of confidence during the home study, it may at first feel hard to admit difficulties. But any experienced social worker knows that all new families have problems and she will be much more worried if you deny them than if you share them freely and plan together about how best to cope. Because the social worker knows you all quite well, but is a little bit detached from your daily affairs, she may well be able to see a pattern in what is happening and have good suggestions about ways to put things right. If additional expert help seems advisable she will know how to obtain this. You are entitled to a good support service from your agency. Make the most of it.

### THE MEANING OF 'ATTACHMENT' AND HOW TO ACHIEVE IT

A major worry for many adoptive parents of an older child is 'Will he ever really belong?' It is a serious question. When you adopt, you do not want a boarder in your house but a new member of the family. For the child, too, it is vital that he should come to feel a true sense of belonging and be deeply attached to your family. Without this family attachment he will be not only physically adrift in the world but also psychologically adrift. We all have to experience attachment before we can become truly independent and good attachment to parents is the basis for sound personal relationships in adult life. There are quite a number of specific things which you can do to build up attachment. Some are rather obvious. Others you will have to think carefully about.

The basic attachment of a baby to his mother occurs when she meets his needs. Baby feels hungry, tense and uncomfortable. Mother feeds him; he is pleasurably full and relaxes. Mother is associated with comfort, and through constant repetition of this pattern attachment develops.

The same pattern can develop with an older child. The child is aroused by strong feelings of discomfort or pleasure and tension builds up. As the need is satisfied or the pleasure experienced, he relaxes again. He becomes attached to those who share this experience. This means that a good time to get close to a child is when he is having an experience that produces strong emotions. Sharing both laughter and tears develops attachment.

Moving into a new family is itself a very emotional experience so the child is particularly open to building new attachments during the early weeks. Other situations which provide special opportunities to develop closeness are helping him to understand his past or come to terms with a worrying or painful experience. Sharing the lost years helps to build bonds. You can be sad together about what you have missed. You can sympathise over the difficult, scary times he had before he came and you can plan to catch up on past experiences. 'When we go to Brighton, we'll show you all the special places we've found.'

Allowing a youngster to regress and be babyish and dependent for a while will help in forming emotional ties as well as giving him the chance to catch up on stages of development he has missed. A spell in bed with the measles or a bad cold will give you a splendid chance to provide the tender loving care that all these youngsters crave even if they cannot show it. We all go back to infancy to some extent when we are ill and the extra attention one gives a sick child may do more for him than cure the cold. You can heal his damaged feelings while you care for his sore throat.

When a child joins a new family it is the responsibility of the adults to help the attachment along. Foster and adoptive parents who complain that their new child is cold and 'didn't help us to love him' have often made the mistake of leaving it to the child to make the first move. They assume, quite wrongly, that the youngster somehow knows that they feel warmly towards him and want him to show affection. This is one of the times when your messages have got to be specially loud and clear.

If you are by nature undemonstrative and find it hard to express your feelings, you are going to have to make a real effort. Your new child needs to hear you say that you love and want him. And not just once but many times because he will find it hard to believe it. He needs to be hugged and kissed. If he shies away and finds it hard to accept, go gently but keep offering affection and find little ways to show that you care.

Supposing, like Vivienne earlier in this chapter, you do not love this little stranger in your midst. What then? Well, you may not love him yet, but you do care about him or you would not have taken him into your home. You can express that care and concern and your hope that he will become your child. Even though there may very well be times when you actively dislike him, there will be other times when your warm feelings come through again and you can make use of these. It may take a very long time before you feel the same about the new child as you do about the existing children in the family, but you can treat them all alike and act fair even when you do not feel fair. This is not acting a lie, it is turning your intentions into actions.

Another important part of developing close bonds is to do nice things together and have fun. Give your child time and attention, encourage him to help with whatever you are doing, share jokes with him and talk about family members, nicknames, events and traditions. Your aim should be to help him move as quickly as possible from feeling an outsider to being an insider. At holiday times when tradition and rituals are to the fore, be sure that he knows what the pattern of the day will be. It will also help to demonstrate your acceptance of the child and his past if you find out whether there have been certain Christmas or birthday rituals that mean a lot to him. If so, incorporate them into your own family pattern.

You can also show your intentions in a very tangible way by having a family photo taken, displaying it in a prominent place and sending copies to your friends in a greeting card.

## COMING THROUGH ON THE OTHER SIDE

This chapter has been mostly about problems. In older child adoptions problems are inevitable and the possibility of failure cannot be ignored. But there is a positive and cheering side too which is well expressed in Claudia Jewett's illuminating book *Adopting the Older Child*. Mrs Jewett and her husband have seven adopted children who came to them at ages ranging from 2 to 17. She writes:

> There is little doubt that this kind of adoption changes everyone involved. Through the immersion in a twenty-four-hour loving, caring, accepting, value-imparting environment, a 'treatment milieu' is created; and demonstrable, lasting healing and change take place in the adopted child. Having found the security of a 'forever' family, the children learn that it is worthwhile to truly care for others. They learn that the risk taken and effort made to become part of a new family are offset by what they have gained. They learn that they are worth loving and caring for;

that they count; that they can control themselves, affect their environment, and solve problems. They can see themselves as unique, important people, capable of bringing happiness to others.

Their parents often come out of the adjustment period feeling that the older child's adoption has been one of the most significant experiences of their lives. They talk about a sense of enormous personal growth, of satisfaction at having sought a meaningful challenge and met it, and of the privilege of having shared something of lasting value with another human being. Most are convinced that the rewards of their adoptions were well worth the hard times, and that they wouldn't have missed out on their experiences for anything.

# CHAPTER XVII

# Bringing up an adopted child

There was once an adopted boy whose parents picked out a delightful mongrel puppy, Skipper, for his eighth birthday present. They had hoped for a smallish dog, but Skipper grew to be very big, bouncy and hard to control. The family all loved him dearly, but the parents finally decided that Skipper would really be happier on a farm than in a small town house.

They talked it over with the little boy, who seemed to agree that would be best for Skipper. An excellent home was found, but when the time came the parents just could not bear to part with the dog. He had become too much part of the family. When the child heard of this change of plan he was almost hysterical with relief. Louise Raymond tells this story in her book *Adoption and After* and goes on to say:

> It was perfectly obvious that way down underneath he had felt that what was going to happen to the dog they had all 'picked out' to come and live with them might, just might, happen to him. What those few weeks took out of the boy is only to be guessed at – and it could have been prevented if the parents had been aware, if they hadn't 'forgotten' their boy was adopted!

This is a good example of the need for adoptive parents to be more than usually aware of possible dangers to their children's security and happiness. It would be most unlikely that a child born into the family would react in this way but an adopted child does not have quite the same certainty about his position. If he has even vague memories of having to leave previous families, he will, of course, be much more likely to get upset by any real or imagined threat to his present security.

Even if they joined their new families in infancy, adopted children are apt to be more than usually liable to feelings of self-doubt, to fears of being different, of failing to reach the standards set by family or friends. All of us suffer from some of these discomforts as we grow up. Most people wish at times that they were better at games, prettier, more popular or got higher marks at school. The adopted child shares these normal anxieties. He also has to learn to live with the fact that he joined his family in a different way, that he once had other parents and that for some reason these parents gave him up.

The child who was older at adoption is likely to remain vulnerable to stress and change and may never quite be able to achieve his full potential. Emotional scars fade, but they seldom disappear completely, and problems are likely to crop up again from time to time as the youngster grows through the various stages of development.

Openness and truthfulness are particularly important to relationships in adoptive families. Adopted children have to accept from their parents the story of how and why they came into the family, so they must have confidence that these parents speak the truth and keep their word. If they have been deceived about other things, they may wonder if they also are being deceived about their adoption story and they may fear that information has been added or withheld. It is wise, for instance, to make it clear that fairy stories are stories and not real life, that Father Christmas is a legend and a symbol, not a living magician.

The same thing applies to the story of where babies come from. It will be confusing enough for your child to learn gradually that he grew in another lady's tummy and has therefore had two mothers, without confusing the issue still more with stories of doctors' bags and gooseberry bushes.

Adoptive parents need to make special efforts to keep open the channels of communication between themselves and their children. They will want their child to feel free to turn to them with questions on any subject, to bring out any doubts or uncertainties, and express his feelings of love or hate or confusion. It is all too easy for parents and children to lose touch with one another's deeper feelings and communicate only on a very superficial level. It is a pity when this happens in any family. When adoption is involved it can lead to trouble.

This does not mean that parents can expect their children to confide in them all the time. Some things they will share more easily with their friends. Most children and young people go through stages when they can talk more easily to adults outside the family. It does not mean that adoptive parents should, so to speak, dig up their children by the roots at intervals to see if they are developing properly. Nor should parents make children the centre of their lives to the exclusion of all outside interests and hobbies. When husband and wife have nothing to talk to one another about except their children's progress or misdeeds it is a danger signal. It does mean that adopters should make special efforts to be available to their children, to have time to talk or share activities or just be there in the background.

SPECIAL CARE AND SPOILING

There is a major difference between giving a child this kind of special care and spoiling him. Spoiling a child is giving him whatever he asks for whether it is good for him or not. It is buying a child's affection or temporary obedience with material gifts, or letting him do as he likes but not caring enough about him to help him learn self-control, consideration for others and how to give as well as take. A child cannot have too much of the genuine love which includes the giving of time, interest and training. He can easily have too much of the selfish, false kind that smothers growth, uses the child for the adult's own gratification, and makes him selfish without giving him any real satisfaction.

If adoptive parents have one general failing it is being over-indulgent and giving the child too many 'things' in an effort to make certain of his affection. They often say when their child is difficult, 'I can't understand why he's like this. We've given him everything.' Sometimes they have showered the child with presents to try to hide their unconscious rejection and relieve their sense of guilt about it. More often it is because they are unsure of themselves as parents and are haunted by the fear that they are not doing as well by the child as his original mother and father would have done. They are afraid their child will think this too if they deny him the things that he asks for.

Adoptive parents who have not been able to come to terms with their infertility sometimes feel that they tried to have children and failed, and are therefore lesser parents who may fail in the upbringing of a child as well. Then they try too hard to be good parents, and do not trust their instincts to be firm or loving or angry.

There is nothing bad about being an adopted child as long as one is loved and wanted. We know from a variety of research studies that most adopted children have happy homes and devoted parents, and grow up to be responsible and successful individuals. Many 'home-grown' children are much less fortunate. Thus there is no need to try to make up to an adopted child for the supposed misfortune of his situation. Parents who feel this way have not yet accepted adoption as something good for them and their child.

The idea that he is in some way peculiar or to be pitied is to be avoided, for it can damage a youngster's self-confidence. You need to be on the lookout for this attitude in well-meaning but uninformed friends and relatives. Such phrases as 'Don't you worry about being adopted,' or 'Nobody will think the worse of you because you're adopted,' can plant an insidious doubt in the child's mind and undo much of your careful teaching and preparation. On the other hand, you may be surprised to hear that your child is getting sympathy and extra attention by telling people he is adopted!

Sometimes adoptive parents feel guilty when they find themselves getting angry with the child they so longed to adopt. There is no need to be. Children are aggravating, naughty and destructive. It is human and natural to be angry. Sometimes the anger is justified, sometimes it is not, and children have to learn that parents are human too. But just as you must accept the fact that you will not be cheerful, fair and patient every day, and may occasionally even feel like shaking your child till his teeth rattle in his head, so you must accept his occasional outbursts of rage and hostility. Sometimes he will feel like hitting or kicking or shouting rude remarks. You really love your youngster even when you are furious with him. He still loves you underneath even when he calls you a mean old pig or declares that you never understand.

Carl and Helen Doss write from much experience:

As your child grows up, it is well to remember that things will not go smoothly any more than they would if your child had been born to you. If you remember that upsets, frustrations, unjust blaming, and sudden angers are a part of normal family life, you will not go to pieces under them, thinking that adoption is the fault. If you can keep your own perspective and be philosophical about the storms and stresses when they come, knowing that they occur in any family, your child will accept the fact too. He will not torment himself by believing that all his troubles would vanish if he were being raised by his 'own' parents.

One of the hardest things for an adoptive parent to take is the tearful accusation, 'If I had my real mother and father, they wouldn't treat me like you do!'

This is not the time to point out that his first parents undoubtedly would have made far more unsatisfactory parents. It is rather a time to acknowledge his feelings. You can say, 'I know just how you feel. When my parents used to get after me about something when I was your age, I simply hated them. I thought that any parents would treat me better than my own did. That's very natural, but I used to get over it, and so will you. All children wish they had a different set of parents when they are angry or cannot have their way.'

It is quite common for any child to imagine at times that these unsympathetic clods are not his real parents. Somewhere, he daydreams, his real parents are waiting for him. They are of finer stuff, of course: perhaps they are a king and queen in a palace, or fabulously wealthy and attractive, living graceful lives in a mansion.

A natural child knows all the time that this is but a fantasy; the danger is that an adopted child might not recognise a fantasy for what it is. He may actually believe that it might be true . . .

Fantasies are best conquered by reality. If the reality of your love and understanding remains constant and concrete, no matter how he may occasionally taunt you with his wishing he had never been adopted, he will not develop any lasting desire to break away from this, his real family.

If he realizes that his feelings are the normal ones of any growing child, adopted or not – that natural children feel the necessity to rebel against authority as part of their maturing – the fantasies will begin to fade.

It is good to remember too that most of the big and little problems that occur in adopted families occur in all families. If some adopted children are rather sensitive, even more adoptive parents tend to be unduly worried and blame themselves unnecessarily. You do not need to fear being compared with the imagined 'real' parents. These taunts are handy weapons. Almost every adopted child uses them from time to time and yours probably will too. He will soon give them up if he finds that you do not rise to the bait, get upset or give in on the point at issue.

Another cause for anxiety among adoptive parents is when they find themselves loving some of their children more than others. This is not a phenomenon of adoption. It happens in many families. Often it is a passing phase and the child who has a period of being very difficult and unlovable grows through it and relationships once more become close and affectionate. Sometimes the difference in feeling is more lasting. There is no need to torment yourself about it for it is a fact of life. All you can do is to build on the positive aspects of your relationship with the child that is harder to love and make sure that you always act fairly even if your feelings are a little different.

 SHOULD YOU TELL OTHER PEOPLE?

If you adopt a child of a different race, your status as an adoptive family will be evident. If there is no such obvious difference, you can choose whom to tell about it. Some parents tell everyone they meet out of pride in the child. Some tell about it in a rather twisted way because they do not wish to acknowledge the youngster as theirs by birth. These are the people who always introduce their child by saying, 'Not my own, you know. We adopted him as a baby.' Imagine how you would feel if you were the child!

Adoption is one part of your private family life. Like other quite intimate things, it will be known to your close friends and relations. If you stay on in the same neighbourhood many people will naturally know. If you should move, there is no reason to tell everyone and no reason to make yourselves uncomfortable trying to hide it.

It will always be wise to tell your family doctor. If you adopt an older child, you should explain the situation to his teacher as, at first, he is likely to be backward at lessons and may well have trouble in getting adjusted to school. Apart from this, there seems no particular reason to mention adoption to a day-school teacher, though you may want to tell the headmaster or headmistress. The head of any boarding school your child attends should be told since he will be responsible for much of your child's upbringing and you will not be on the spot to deal with any problems which may arise. If you do not feel certain that he will use this knowledge wisely, then he is not a good person to entrust with your adopted child's care.

As far as other friends and acquaintances go, there is no need to mention adoption unless it seems appropriate and you would feel more comfortable if you did so. If your youngster is inclined at first to tell his adoption story all over the neighbourhood, you may wish to explain to him that this is a sort of nice family secret. Later he too will tell people just when he feels it would be suitable and comfortable to do so.

If your child looks very much like you or has similar manner-isms, and adopted children often have a startling resemblance to their parents, you can fully agree when people remark on it. If he is of the same race but happens to look very different from you, people may comment, 'Your boy certainly doesn't take after you in looks, does he?' If this happens, you may be able to think of some way in which the child resembles a relative or close family friend so that you can say something like, 'No, but he reminds us so much of my Uncle John', or 'He seems to share his grand-father's skill with a paint-brush.' This will help your youngster understand that you like the way he looks and feel he is a worthy and acceptable member of your whole family circle.

## IF YOU ARE NOW AN INTER-RACIAL FAMILY

Jan Knott, the mother of one white 'home grown' and two black adopted children has written helpfully about how it must feel for a black child to grow up in a white family:

> Before any child can take his place in the world with spirit and confidence he must feel good about himself; he must feel loved. If he is black this pride must include pride in the colour of his skin.
>
> A black child growing up in a black family doesn't know he's learning to feel good about being black. He doesn't think about his skin any more than a white child does. He knows his mum and dad love him the way he is and he wants to be just like them.
>
> But for the black child growing up in a white community, life is immediately more complex and self-conscious. Those of us who are white have grown up with whiteness as a norm. When caring for a black child we have to learn to see things as the child sees them.
>
> People may tell you that a child doesn't notice his skin colour but this is untrue. Children do notice . . . If we are embarrassed to mention his colour approvingly, the child is going to grow up associating open mention of his colour only with playground name calling. If we think it's not polite to

refer to his blackness, he may think it's not polite to *be* black.

A black child in a predominently white world may not feel 'odd' he may feel 'wrong'. Everything tells him that it's better to be white, and it is a sad but true reflection that black children will often draw themselves as white.

So how do we redress the balance? There are many simple, positive things we can do, starting with caring properly for the child's personal appearance.

Jan goes on to talk about the importance of grooming, including learning to braid hair properly or manage an attractive 'Afro'. Do not be shy of asking a black adult for help. Black people groom their own children beautifully and will be glad you want to do the same. Hair cream, oil for the skin and extra vitamins are all necessary for the black child.

Providing play things and books that reflect a multi-cultural society is important too. Jan tells how her black children almost always choose books that include pictures of black children or, better still, have a black child as the hero or heroine.

We know from black people who have grown up in white homes that it will be difficult, probably impossible for your black son or daughter to talk with you about what it feels like to be on the receiving end of racial prejudice. The black child in a black family knows his parents have the same experience. Your child will realise that this is something which you cannot fully share and he may feel disloyal to you in even raising the subject. Nor can you teach him the survival techniques that he will need to develop. To learn these he will have to look to black adults and other black children. You can best help by making sure that he has the opportunity to know black people. This is much more easily achieved if you live in a racially mixed neighbourhood. If yours is an all-white area, you will have to plan and work specially hard to make sure that your growing child, and especially your growing teenager, has the opportunities he will need to mix with black people, find his own identity and learn how to be strong in the face of pressure and discrimination.

Some discrimination there is almost bound to be no matter where you live. While the young black child is usually easily accepted, even over-indulged, the black teenager is likely to have more trouble. There can be hurt and humiliation for a black boy when his white girl friend's parents disapprove of him. The black girl in a white community may find that she is not asked out on dates or that the local boys all assume that she must be 'hot stuff' because black people are believed to be highly sexed.

Schools still tend to teach only British history, and all too often African, Asian and West Indian nations appear in our history books as ignorant, subject peoples being brought the benefits of Western civilisation through the British Empire. Their own interesting early civilisations are ignored along with their more recent achievements and famous men and women. It will therefore be up to you to introduce your black child to the history of his country of origin so that he can understand and be proud of his roots as well as of his British citizenship.

National dishes and the rituals associated with meals are an interesting and important part of everyone's cultural heritage. If you take trouble to cook and serve some ethnic foods and incorporate some appropriate customs or rituals into your family's daily life, this will demonstrate in a small but effective way that you accept and admire your child's background. You will be answering in actions as well as in words the question Jan Knott's little black daughter often asks: 'I like you white. Do you like me black?'

ADOPTED CHILDREN IN ADOLESCENCE

Teenagers are most provoking creatures. Their behaviour is often puzzling, annoying and hard to live with. Most parents, adoptive and otherwise, have their understanding, patience and humour stretched to the limit by their adolescent children's unpredictable and trying ways. But if this is a difficult period for the adult members of the family it is an equally hard time for the young people themselves. How many of us would really like to go back to our teens? Can't we all remember the shyness and clumsiness, the feeling of self-doubt or inferiority, the discomfort of being neither a child nor an adult and ill at ease with both groups.

There are good reasons for many of the common problems that arise at this age, and it may help both the youngsters and their distracted parents to know that they are not alone in their troubles. Adolescence is not a disease, but the final and perhaps the most difficult stage of the long journey from infancy to maturity. It is a half-way house, and like most temporary housing it is uncomfortable and full of snags. A wise psychiatrist once said that the best cure for adolescent troubles is seven years.

Physically the adolescent is going through a period of rapid change and growth. A boy may seem to change almost overnight from a compact, well co-ordinated little fellow to a gangling, lanky youth who trips over people's feet, drops everything he touches and has always outgrown his clothes.

Boys and girls, conscious of these bodily changes and scared of the new feelings and urges that accompany them, are often painfully self-conscious and shy. To be unusually tall, short or heavy, to have pimples or be wearing the wrong sort of clothes for the occasion can seem an overwhelming tragedy to a teenager.

During the troublous years from 12 to 20 each individual has to establish himself as a person in his own right apart from his family. He must learn to stand on his own feet, choose a career, start to make up his mind about his beliefs, standards of conduct and ambitions for life. It is not surprising if during this process he swings from one extreme to the other, one day seeming more babyish than a 6-year-old and the next asserting 'I can manage my own affairs, thank you.' If he is to learn to be independent, he probably has to rebel sometimes; if he is to make up his own mind about what he thinks, he has to challenge accepted beliefs and practices and try out new ideas. To some extent each new generation has to break away from the old in order to establish itself. Each in turn complains that adults do not understand, while for their part the bemused parents feel that in their own youth their behaviour was never so outrageous. These days, the rapid changes in social and sexual behaviour make the generation gap seem specially great.

Telling about two of her foster children, Mrs Rose writes in *Room For One More*:

> Some years before when Jane had indulged in a temper outburst, Joey followed me into the kitchen and asked, 'Oh Mother! Why does she talk so cross to you?
>
> 'She's just adolescent, I guess,' I answered cheerfully, whereupon he put his short arms as far around my wide waist as they would go and cried, 'Mother, I promise, I promise that I'll never, never be adolescent.'
>
> And yet, in spite of his vow, he was! All of a sudden, one Thursday morning, for no reason at all he sat quietly crying into his breakfast cereal. Joey, who was always so cheerful, so energetic and affectionate, turned, overnight, into a tearful, moody, lazy stranger. That was the time when I really did worry about heredity! 'Do you suppose he has insanity somewhere in his family?' I asked my husband, but he only laughed.

'It's just a temporary insanity,' he assured me. 'They all get it, and they all get over it. It's only adolescence. You'd better not collapse under this case of it. There are a few more coming up!'

That period of 'temporary insanity' was very wearing.

While all parents share these problems and are perplexed, worried and exasperated at times, adoptive parents are inclined to be more so and are apt to blame adoption for problems that are a normal part of adolescence. Like Mrs Rose they may wonder whether some hereditary mental illness or unpleasant characteristics are now coming out in the child. Or they may, quite unnecessarily, blame themselves for failing to become the perfect parents they set out to be.

In face of the adolescent's bewildering variations of mood, the rapid changes in friends and interests, the unexpected reactions and enthusiasms, parents naturally wonder what has happened to their child's personality. The little boy or girl they thought they understood so well seems to have disappeared. A great many parents have felt at times that 'this youngster does not seem like any child of ours.' Those whose children are adopted wonder whether adoption accounts for these differences.

The personality of the adolescent is not fixed. He is, as it were, trying on various characteristics for size. He is outwardly challenging his parents' standards and the conventions of their social group, although underneath he may be very loyal to them. In order to find out what sort of people he likes, he may make a wide variety of friends from different walks of life; he may go through a period of thinking it grown up and clever to tell off-colour jokes; most adolescents like to wear clothes that their older relatives consider unsuitable or unattractive; few girls use make-up discreetly or sensibly at first. These are typical characteristics of teenagers and in no way peculiar to adopted children.

There may, however, be extra growing up problems for some adopted adolescents. Those who had 'special needs' as younger children may have them still as teenagers. It is in adolescence that the full meaning of some handicaps becomes evident and much love and help will be needed as the youngster tries to face the future. The young black person who has been brought up in a white family may have a particularly difficult task in fusing his dual heritage into a comfortable identity. The child who joined the family late after a difficult early life, may well go through another rough passage in his teens. As part of the normal growing up process, adolescents often go back to earlier stages of development. This can have its trying aspects, but it does provide an opportunity to work at the problems again so the youngster can come though to a healthy maturity.

Adopted adolescents have a particular need to feel accepted as individuals in their own right. Parents can help a lot by taking their teenager's suggestions and ideas seriously even if they do not agree with them and by giving him suitable freedom and responsibility. At the same time they can stand firm behind him to set necessary limits and provide a secure base from which he can venture out on his own.

While they should be alive to the possibility of quite fundamental personality differences between themselves and their child, adoptive parents should also beware of thinking that an unsuitable friendship or love affair, a craze for lurid romances, or an overwhelming ambition to become a film star are signs of hereditary instability, low breeding or poor upbringing. They are more likely a very temporary phase which will soon be outgrown.

Adults working or living with teenagers do well to look back sympathetically to their own youthful efforts to grow up. They should try to judge each incident or problem as part of the adolescent's whole personality and development, and also against the wider background of local teenage customs and habits. Many a worried parent has been relieved to find that other parents have just the same problems or that their youngster is merely following a typical teenage craze. It can be most reassuring to find that the teacher considers your child a perfectly well-behaved and normal member of the group. Some people find books by educators, psychiatrists and other parents a help, but your best assets will be common sense, stamina and a sense of humour.

# CHAPTER XVIII

# Explaining adoption

In the early days when adoption first became popular, it was taken for granted that as far as possible it would be kept secret. Some people went to fantastic lengths to make it seem that their children had been born to them. But as some of the disastrous effects of secrecy became more widely known this attitude changed. Now almost everyone agrees that children should be told if they are adopted. The question is how and when.

The most obvious reason why adoptive parents must explain is that their children will find out anyway. But there is more to it than this. Happiness and security cannot be built on lies or fears of discovery.

Even though they had no conscious memory of another home, some adopted children have had a vague feeling that they belonged to their family in a different way. Many more have overheard chance remarks and conversations that made them wonder. Another child or an unthinking adult may carelessly or in anger declare, 'That's not your real mother, you know,' or 'I wonder why your parents didn't send you back to the adoption people when they found out what they got.'

If your child's first knowledge of his adoption comes in such a way, it will be hard to convince him that adoption is something good. The well-prepared youngster can fire back with the retort, 'Well, your mother had to take you. My parents chose to have me.' The child who does not know the truth is defenceless. Parents may not be there at the right moment to offer help and protection.

Almost everyone who has much to do with adoptions knows one or two dismal stories of children who were seriously disturbed by the sudden discovery that they were adopted. Carol, an attractive, intelligent 16-year-old, went out to a party at a friend's house. Through an open door she heard two adults talking about her. 'Such a pretty girl,' said one, 'you'd never think she was an abandoned baby when they adopted her, would you?' Carol fled from the party and rushed home to demand the truth. There was a terrible scene and Carol left home. She made it up with her adoptive parents later, but their relationship was never quite the same again, for she felt they had deceived her for many years.

A less extreme case was that of Martin. He was 9 when a boy down the street teased him about being adopted. Martin stoutly denied it and hurried home to ask his parents. He burst into the kitchen where his mother, hot and flustered, was dishing up the Sunday dinner for a family party. 'Peter Brown says I'm adopted. But I'm not, am I?' he asked. His mother took the easy road out and answered quickly, 'No, dear, of course not.'

Martin was satisfied for the moment but he did not forget. After a while he remembered other things, too, and how his Aunt Jenny had once talked about the day his parents fetched him from the nursery. He had not thought much of it at the time but now it seemed peculiar. He knew babies grew inside their mothers. Finally, overcome by curiosity, he looked in the box where his mother kept all her papers. There he found his adoption certificate. 'Where were you when I was born?' he asked his mother one day. And another time, 'why was I in the nursery when you brought me home?' Having lied once, his mother did not like to admit the truth. Each time she uneasily brushed aside Martin's questions and his unspoken plea for help and explanations.

Sensing his parent's discomfort, Martin was afraid to tell of his discovery, but his confusion and unhappiness were reflected in his behaviour, which suddenly became quite different. He was rude, defiant, refused to come home on time and even played truant from school. His parents, who were devoted to him, could now do nothing with him.

It was finally to an understanding teacher that Martin sobbed out his discovery, his fear that there must be something dreadfully bad about being adopted or why would his parents not tell him, and the even worse fear that this was not really his home so he might be sent away any time.

When his parents realised what they had unknowingly done to their child they tried their very best to help. They explained that they had not told him before for fear of hurting him; they told how much they had wanted a little boy and how he was just the sort of boy they wanted to be theirs 'for always'. They talked about it many times and gradually Martin settled down again, though it was many months before he fully regained his cheerful confidence.

How different is the story of Jack, who remarked to his mother one day, 'Robert said you're not my real Mum. The cheek of it! After all, I was only born to that first mother.'

Adoptive parents who try to hide the fact of adoption or who postpone the telling until the child is a member of the community live in constant dread that the youngster will discover the truth. Every day they fear that he will find out or suspect and ask awkward questions; every month it becomes harder to break the silence, more difficult to know how to begin to explain. Such a secret is almost bound to form a barrier between parent and child. It creates all kinds of problems and anxieties which need not exist.

WHY IT IS HARD TO TELL

It is very easy to talk glibly about the need to tell children about their adoption. This does not make it any easier to do. Most adoptive parents feel so close to their children and love them so much that it is hard to remember and admit that these children were not born to them. Many parents rather dread the telling and wish it were not necessary. Sometimes it stirs painful recollections of infertility. Adopters are aware of the deep emotional meaning of adoption both for themselves and for their children. In just the same way many people feel a little tense and embarrassed when they first start giving their youngsters information about sex and intimate personal relationships.

One day Muriel Martin was telling her close friend, Marjorie, about her fear that if they told their little daughter, Angela, she was not born to them she would love them less. Suddenly Marjorie said, 'Were you related to Donald before your marriage?' 'Why, no,' said Muriel, surprised, 'why do you ask that?' Instead of answering direct, Marjorie asked another question. 'Look, Muriel,' she said, 'you and Donald are related to one another by love and choice, not by blood. Why do you expect Angela to be upset or to love you less when she hears that you adopted her to complete your family and be your daughter?'

Muriel went home and thought about this conversation. She

talked it over with her husband too. After a while they realised that because they had had some doubts and fears they had assumed Angela would too. In fact, they were good parents and Angela was a happy, affectionate child.

To their immense relief, Angela was proud and delighted when they told her the story of her adoption. She boasted about it at her kindergarten class. Unlike the rest, she was not only born, she was adopted, and that was 'special'. Some of the other children wished they were adopted too!

## HOW WILL THE CHILD FEEL ABOUT IT?

In the long run children feel much the same way about their adoption as their parents do. If you are happy with your adopted child he will sense this and be content with his status.

Sometimes it is difficult for adults to put themselves in a child's place and to remember that children do not start with any pre-conceived ideas about a situation. Telling is much more of a problem for the parents than for the young child, to whom it generally seems perfectly ordinary and natural. However, the things children most want to know about are not always just what we would expect.

To begin with, most adopted children are less interested in how their parents came to take them than in whether they are glad they did. When a child asks about his natural parents he may not want facts about them so much as answers to the questions, 'Was it because there was something wrong with me that they gave me away?' 'Need I be ashamed of my origins?' 'Might I lose this home too?'

Because the answers could be so frightening, very few children will ask questions outright. Parents need to have a third ear for what their youngsters are really trying to say. Often it helps to ask the child to explain a little more. For instance, if he asks, 'Are you my real mummy and daddy?' you can say, 'Do you mean, are you our boy for always and always?' He very likely does want this reassurance. But he might be trying to ask, 'Was I born to you?' It will be important for you to know which so that you can sort out his confusions or calm his fears.

In the same way, when an older child asks why his parents gave him up, he may be even more interested in knowing that they thoughtfully decided this would be best for him than in the actual reasons for their decision. At some stage almost all adopted children want to know facts about their first parents and what lies behind their adoption. To be curious about one's origins is natural and right. For many youngsters the curiosity is casual or short lived; others do go through periods of deep concern and need a lot of information, help and support to get it all straight. This seems to be largely a matter of temperament.

## WHEN AND HOW TO START EXPLAINING

There is not any one perfect moment to start the adoption story just as there is no one perfect way to tell it. Much depends on personal preference. If you should be adopting a second child while your first is still young, this can be a good starting-point. If a neighbour or relative is having a baby this can give you an opportunity to talk about birth and adoption. There has to be some moment when you take the plunge. Remember, too, that telling is your responsibility. You cannot wait for your child to make the first move.

Often people talk about telling a child 'when he is old enough to understand.' In practice, this does not make much sense. He will not be able to understand some of it till he is in his teens. Some things he will not fully understand until he is adult and has a family of his own. Some he can grasp while he is still very little. Research studies have confirmed that it is almost always best if parents make sure that the child knows he is adopted before he starts school.

Telling about adoption is not a once-and-forever affair. It is a gradual and repeated process. Much of the explaining is done just by living and loving. Some of it has to be put into words. At first the prospect of 'going through all this' many times may seem daunting. It can also be reassuring. If you do not make a very good job of it the first time there will be other times. If you miss a good opportunity or fail to understand what your child is really asking or wanting, there will be other chances.

Hopefully you have decided not to risk waiting until your child is mature before you tell him. There is, therefore, much to be said for starting very early. Then there will never be a time when he did not know he was adopted. It can never be a shock to him. Another advantage is that it gives you a chance to practise. You can get used to telling the story out loud.

When you feel particularly happy and loving you might give your toddler a kiss or a hug saying 'I'm so glad we adopted you.' In this way he will begin to associate early on the word adopted with love and pleasure.

The word 'chosen' is often used to describe an adopted child but can backfire. The idea that you chose to adopt as you chose to marry is helpful. But the idea that he was picked out from a row of babies could make your child feel that he has to live up to impossibly high expectations or that if you are disappointed in your choice, you might send him back. It is also almost certainly untrue and it is a mistake to allow untruths to distort and complicate the story. You may like to explain that the adoption agency chose you to be his 'forever parents' because they knew he would be happy with you and that you could provide the sort of home that his birth mother wanted him to have.

Children learn gradually about many things. They ask questions until their parents are almost distracted, but at first they don't need very complicated answers. When a 3-year-old asks, 'What makes an aeroplane fly?' he is content with the reply 'It has wings, and a motor inside like a car.' Later he will want many more details and may become interested in different types of aircraft, engine construction etc. When a 4-year-old asks, 'Why don't little girls look the same as boys when they undress?' he will be satisfied for the time being with, 'Girls are growing up to be mummies and boys are growing up to be daddies. They are born different.' Later, of course, he will want much more information about the physical and emotional aspects of sex.

In the same way you will want to gear your explanations of adoption to your child's age, understanding, and what he needs to know at each stage of his development. Children vary in this as they do about most things, but parents should beware of thinking that lack of questions means lack of curiosity. If a child senses that his parents are tense and anxious about such subjects as sex or adoption, he will find it very difficult to ask questions even if he really needs the answers. The more affectionate and sensitive the child, the harder he will find it to risk upsetting his parents with awkward questions.

When Robin asked 'What was the mummy that borned me like?' his mother burst into tears. Robin, a loving 6-year-old, was immediately repentant. 'Darling Mummy I promise, I promise I'll never ask you again' he said. How sad that this little boy should have to take on the burden of anxiety that there is something so upsetting about his background that he must never ask about if for fear of distressing his much-loved mother! Her tears would not have mattered if she could have shown him that she understood his need to ask the question. Many adopters and children have felt all the better for having a good cry together and there is both pain and joy in the adoptive situation.

If your child does not say anything about adoption for long periods, it may be that he feels it would be disloyal to you to ask, so it is up to you to open up the subject again. You can do it very casually and he may not want to pursue the subject. If that is the case, nothing will be lost. But by providing the opportunity you will have made it clear that if and when he has questions, you will try to provide answers and that talking about his birth parents is all right.

In Lois Raynor's study of adoption *The Adopted Child Comes of Age* many adoptees, now young adults, spoke of how much they wished their parents had been willing and able to give them more information about their first families. Quite often their adoptive parents had told them they were adopted and left it at that. They had left the job half done since getting across the fact of adoption is only the first step. It is, however, an important step. Just what you say is not too important. It is the feeling behind the words that counts.

Some parents use the bed-time story method. They may start, gradually with stories of animals and then lead into the story of a mother and father who wanted a little boy or girl, and how they looked and looked till they found one they could have to be their very own. Other parents start right away with the story that most children love above all others because it is about themselves. It is not difficult to weave a story round your wish for a child but you could not grow one of your own so you visited the lady who 'knows all about babies'. She found you just the sort of baby you had always wanted. Details of the journey home, the buying of toys, baby food etc. all make interesting telling. Every story will of course be a little different and can be illustrated by the family scrap-book or photograph album. All children love to hear about when they were little, and adoptive parents can make use of this interest. If you include in your family album or child's special book some details of his first family it will help make the explanations much easier. You may have a letter from the adoption agency that could be included and shared with him later to give some factual information about his background.

A farmer and his wife adopted a family of three small children who had been abandoned by their very young mother and had then spent time in a residential nursery. They found that lambing time gave them an ideal opportunity to explain several aspects of adoption. They took the children with them when they went to pick up the lambs which had been born to very young ewes – too young and inexperienced to be good mothers. Some lambs were introduced carefully to ewes who had no lambs or were experienced enough to look after an extra one. A few they brought to the farmhouse to be reared by hand until they were strong enough to join a sheep family. The children were able to see how this was like what had happened to them.

There are now a number of good books about adoption written for children of different ages. Some of them are listed at the end of this chapter. British Agencies for Adoption and Fostering has an excellent, inexpensive pamphlet called 'Explaining Adoption' which any adoptive parent will benefit from reading, and also provides lists of books and leaflets on adoption. It can be a great help to talk to other adoptive parents. Many agencies hold discussion groups for their past adopters and of course the Parent to Parent Information on Adoption Services meetings are an excellent place to meet other adoptive families. PPIAS meetings also provide opportunities for adopted children to meet and thus to combat any feelings of isolation or difference.

A child cannot really begin to understand adoption until he learns where babies come from and that he was not born into your family. Therefore, when he starts asking questions, and he is likely to do this between the ages of 3 and 6, it is wise to start immediately giving simple, truthful answers. This does not mean that you must embark on explanations in a bus queue or shop; children only too often ask at the most awkward moments! There is no harm in saying 'We'll talk about it when we get home.' But if you have to put off answering, it will be up to you to raise the question again later. If you find it hard to talk about sexual matters there are helpful books on this subject too. Some are for you to read to your child, some you can give him to read to himself as he gets older. It would be a pity to rely entirely on books, however, as discussion of important and intimate matters like adoption and sex is one of the ways in which a family draws closer.

When a child asks his first questions about adoption or where babies come from, it is sometimes a temptation to sit the child down and tell him the whole story at once in an effort to get it over. This is not a good idea. It is better to leave the child free to ask about what's puzzling him. Parents who do all the talking do not know what their child is thinking about or how much he understands. Giving information before a child is ready may cause unnecessary confusion and difficulty and if he is not ready for it he cannot absorb it. Something as complicated and important as adoption or sex has to be told several times. It is quite common for children to forget and confuse what they are told. Sometimes they get very strange ideas indeed. There is no need for alarm about this. Given time and patient, truthful explanations, the child will get it straightened out in the end.

Just as most adoptive parents wish very much that their child had been born to them, so children sometimes wish they had been born to their adoptive parents. If your child says he wishes he had grown in your tummy, you can answer truthfully that you wish so too but that what makes a mother is not just growing babies in tummies but loving and caring and enjoying things together. It is important to get this idea across clearly because it provides the child with an answer to any taunts that you are not his 'real' mother because you did not 'grow' him. This is one of the aspects of adoption which may need to be talked through several times.

Most children go through a period of thinking one is either born or adopted and they need help in understanding. This generally brings up the question, 'Do I have another mother?' At this point some adoptive parents begin to feel at a loss. It is natural to feel some envy of the woman who was able to bear your child, but it is unwise to let the child sense any ill-feeling against his birth mother. In fact, the less he 'feels' about her at this point the better, though he must know that she existed. You are his real mother now, his 'always' mother.

When talking to a very young child it may be best not to call his natural parents mother and father unless he does so himself. You can say that he grew in another lady's tummy, that she could not keep him, and as you and daddy wanted a baby so much he became your boy.

Later your child will need to understand that he once had another mother and father, but it is always wise to avoid using the expressions 'your own mother' or 'your real mother'. Even 'your other mother' makes it sound as if the child has two mothers, whereas he only has you. One good way to put it is 'your first mother'. There is no emotional feeling about the word 'first'. The child knows 'first' as something which comes and goes. He has experienced his first tooth, his first day at school, his first bicycle. You may also find the expression 'birth mother and father' quite useful.

It is hard for many people to understand how a mother can give up her baby. Adopted children find this difficult to understand too, especially now that there are so many single-parent families.

They sometimes think that there must have been something wrong with them that made them unwanted. Some adopters have felt it best to say that the natural parents are dead. It seems to solve the problem but it does not really because later the child will wonder about his other relatives and why they did not take him. Then, too, if you say his parents are sick or dead, your child may be frightened every time you get flu and panic-stricken if you should have an operation. He may fear that you will also die and leave him. Rather similar difficulties can occur if you say, 'They were too poor to take care of you.' Family money troubles or talk about the high cost of living can come to have a fearful meaning for a child.

In adoption, as in other life situations, honesty is the best principle. Usually the reasons for adoption are not too difficult to explain but sometimes there will be aspects which a child could not cope with or comprehend. You may not want to give all the details at once, but you certainly want to avoid having to contradict or deny previous statements, so do not give inaccurate information even to a young child. At first it may be sufficient to say 'They had grown-up problems and just couldn't look after you,' but as he gets older even painful truths will be more bearable than doubts and uncertainty. When we do not know something we are all apt to imagine the worst.

Maybe you were unlucky in that your adoption agency did not give you any written information and you have now forgotten some of the things they told you about your child's background. Maybe they did give it to you, but you have lost the paper and now your child is asking questions and you wish you had the answers for him. If this happens, you should not hesitate to go back for more information. Adoption agencies are now obliged to keep their records for fifty years so, although the social worker you knew has very likely left, someone there can look things up for you. If your adoption society has closed down, their records will have been taken over by another agency. British Agencies for Adoption and Fostering will very likely be able to tell you where your society's records are now held.

ADOLESCENTS AND NATURAL PARENTS

By the time an adopted child reaches his teens he should, of course, know that he was adopted and have some elementary sex education. Now he will begin to be interested in more than the basic facts. He will want to know about feelings. He will question motives and seek to deepen his understanding of himself and other people. Adoptive parents have an important job to do here.

If you have achieved a sympathetic understanding of your child's birth parents and the reasons why they placed him for adoption, then you will be able to convey this to him. It will, of course, be a help if you have met them and can give some first-hand impressions, but in any case you can pass on what you learned about them from your social worker. You can also help him to be grateful to his birth parents for the gift of life.

The possibility that your sympathetic explanations of the natural parents' actions will conflict with the moral teaching and standards of behaviour you are trying to uphold is not such a problem as it seems at first sight. Nor is it peculiar to adopted children. We all have to learn that we can have compassion for other less fortunate people without copying their behaviour. An adopted teenager can be helped to understand illegitimacy without feeling humiliated or unworthy. Your attitudes will be vital here. Your child needs to know that his origins are acceptable to you. If he senses evasion or discomfort whenever the subject comes up, or if there seems to be a great gulf between his past and present families, it will be more difficult for him to feel a complete person and comfortable with his adoptive status.

There is a fairly narrow path to tread between turning natural parents into the loving, wonderful, wealthy figures of the fairy stories and making them sound no good. It may be helpful to remember that the adopted child who has never known his first parents can have no feeling of closeness or love for them. He might build up an idealised picture of them, but he is just as likely to have unnecessary fears that his origins were sordid or shameful. In fact, most adopted children come from respectable everyday families and their natural parents are very ordinary people who got their lives into a muddle.

Most adolescents are day-dreamers and more interested in themselves than anyone else. They are struggling to find their own identity and place in the world. An adopted adolescent has to settle his ideas about his natural parents and it is normal that at times he should be curious about them. Just because he wants to know some facts about his ancestry does not mean that he is dissatisfied with his present home or has any idea of running off to look for his original family. You can meet his needs by giving simple matter-of-fact information about what his first mother and father looked like, their nationality, age, employment and any details you may know about their skills or interests or about other members of their families. Do be sure to include the good things that he can identify with and be proud of. There is no reason to fear that all this information will lead to an unhealthy curiosity. In fact quite the reverse. It is failure to get satisfactory answers that is likely to lead to preoccupation with questions. Your child may go through a stage of being a bit upset about his adoption, but with your help he will grow through it as he has other difficult stages. All adolescents have problems of one kind or another. If it is not adoption it is something else!

The Children Act 1975 has made it possible for adopted people over the age of 18 to get access to their original birth records. Many adoptive parents were worried and upset about this at the time, fearing that large numbers of adopted teenagers would rush to get their original birth certificates.

Experience has shown that these fears were unfounded. Less than two per cent of all adopted people have been taking advantage of the new provision. Rather few of them are teenagers with the largest proportion being in their mid-20s to mid-30s. Of this small number of adoptees seeking their original birth certificates, only a few are interested in trying to find their first parents. When such reunions have proved possible, they seem to have been generally successful in putting minds at rest on both sides, but they have very seldom led to long-term relationships.

You may still feel uneasy about the whole idea and wonder why it was thought necessary to change the law in this way. Perhaps the best way to explain this is to include a statement from an adopted person who is also an adoptive mother and quoted in the BAAF leaflet 'Talking About Origins. An open letter to adoptive parents.'

This is what she says:

> I was adopted as an infant by wonderful parents who couldn't have given me a better home or childhood. We had very little money, but an abundance of everything important. My father died when I was 13, my mother is still living, almost 80, a remarkable and unique person, delightful to know. I am also an adoptive parent, 40 years old, mother of three, very happily married. We adopted the youngest of our children because we wanted at least one more child, and because I wanted to try to do something comparable to what I felt my parents had done for me.
>
> I think in general I have my head on straight. I am happy

with my family and friends, and I think they are happy with me. I have had a lovely life full of lots of fun, love and personal satisfaction. But I have reached that point where I absolutely must know the truth about my origins. I did not feel this need until I had my first child. When I first saw my son I wept, not because he wasn't the most beautiful child God had ever created, which he certainly was, but because he was the first living being I had ever seen to whom I was truly related. It was an overwhelming experience, a kind of total system-shock.

I say this so you will know that this is not always – as a matter of fact is not usually – a teenage identity crisis. A large proportion of us in this position are in our 30s and 40s.

I do not need a new mother, I've got a wonderful one of my own. I do not need a new family – mine is the best there is. I admit to a persistent curiosity about half brothers and sisters, because I was an only child, with an only child's conviction that it would be nice to have someone with whom to share the family joys and problems. I can never, however, expect to find the warm relation of my fantasies, and I know it.

What is it I want then? You who are not adopted cannot know what it is to be shut out of a family's history . . . Who do *I* take after? Is there anyone out there like *me*?

I need to know where I came from so that I can better tell my children where they are going. I want to know who I'm better than or not as good as. Is there someone else before me who was substantially grey at 40, and mildly arthritic? I feel like a middle without a beginning.

When you are dealing with your teenager's concerns about his origins, it is well to realise that many questions which seem to refer to specific details are really an attempt to find out about feelings. When children ask 'Why did my parents give me up?' they often mean 'Was my mother the sort of person you are, or would I be ashamed of her? Did she love me?' You may or may not know the exact answers to his direct questions but you can and must try to answer the unspoken questions, 'Am I an acceptable and lovable person? Is it all right to be an adopted child?' Even if you cannot provide all the facts he would like about his natural family, you can often help by such answers as 'I think your parents were probably rather like us because the agency thought you would fit so well into our family', or 'She must have been a lovely mummy to have had you', or 'I'm sure one of your ancestors must have been good at music (or maths or tennis) because you took to it so easily,' or, if necessary, 'I'm sure she wanted to be a good mother even though she wasn't able to be.' If you cannot satisfy your youngster's curiosity, go back with him to the adoption agency and ask for more information.

Every major piece of research into the outcome of adoption has shown that adopted people regard those who brought them up as their real parents, but that they want to know something of their natural family background and that they feel it is their adoptive parents' responsibility to give them this information. This means that it is up to you to make the first move, to keep the subject open, to provide opportunities for questions and to make it clear that you are willing to try and provide answers.

Curiosity about origins seems to come and go in waves. If your child has not mentioned adoption for some time, you may need to make a casual reference to it. If you get a lot of questions and discussions, don't worry, feel proud that your relationship with the child makes this possible.

Sometimes teenagers need a chance to talk things over with someone outside the immediate family – an aunt or uncle, family friend or trained counsellor. While parents should try to keep open channels of communication with their children, they need not be upset or jealous if the youngster talks more easily with someone else. This too, is a temporary phase. There may be long periods when a teenager never discusses his deeper feelings at all. Then he may suddenly open up with all sorts of confidences.

Adolescence is a difficult, challenging period for parents. It is also a hopeful, exciting and rewarding time. As your son or daughter moves forward with increasing confidence towards maturity and independence, you will feel a glow of well-earned satisfaction. There will no doubt be problems ahead. Life is like that. You cannot spare your child all sorrow, disappointment and frustration. But you will know that the thoughtful care which gave him a secure childhood in a loving family has been the best possible foundation for a happy and successful future.

# USEFUL ADDRESSES

British Agencies for Adoption and Fostering
11 Southwark Street, London, SE1 1RQ

Harmony
42 Beech Drive, Boreham Wood, Herts., WD6 4QU

National Association for the Childless
318 Summer Lane, Birmingham, B19 3RL

National Foster Care Association
Francis House, Francis Street, London, SW1P 1DE

Parent to Parent Information on Adoption Services
26 Belsize Grove, London, NW3 4T3

Voluntary Council for Handicapped Children
8 Wakley Street, London, EC1V 7QE

# FURTHER READING

**BOOKS**

Infertility
*Infertility*, Consumers Association, 1969.
*Infertile Marriage*, Robert Newill, Penguin, 1974.
*Why Us?*, Andrew Stanway, Granada, 1980.

Adopting and Fostering
*Adopting The Older Child*, Claudia Jewett, Harvard Common Press, 1978.
*Our Four Boys – Foster Parenting Retarded Teenagers*, Syracuse University Press, 1978.

For Children
*Why Was I Adopted?*, Carole Livingstone, Angus & Robertson, 1978.
*Jane Is Adopted*, Althea, Dinosaur Publications, 1980.
*David And His Sister Carol*, Althea, Dinosaur Publications, 1976.
*Mr Fairweather And His Family*, Kornitzer, Bodley Head, 1960.

If you cannot find them in your library or local bookshop, these books can all be ordered by post from: Bookstall Services, 86 Abbey Street, Derby, DE3 3SQ.


**PAMPHLETS AND LEAFLETS**

(available from British Agencies for Adoption and Fostering, 11 Southwark Street, London, SE1 IRQ)

Adopting A Child
Explaining Adoption
Meeting Children's Needs Through Adoption and Fostering
If You Are Adopted (For young adoptees)
Talking About Origins (An open letter to adoptive parents)
Getting To Know You (A picture book for people adopting older children)

# INDEX

access, to original birth records, 180

activities, need to prepare for visits, 106, 126

adopted children: in adolescence, 165–8; curiosity about origins, 172–3, 175–6, 179–82; insecurity in, 157–8; need for information, 169–71; research on, 68–9, 160

adoption agencies, 93–8

adoption allowances, 11, 40

Adoption Exchange Service, 94

adoption parties, 99–100

adoption records, 178, 180

age: gap between children, 19–20, 22; of prospective adopters, 33

agreements to adoption, 11, 87–8

alcoholism: inheritance of, 69

anger: of adopters, 160; of child, 145–6, 160

attachment, 153–4

babies: moving into new families, 119–20, 124–7, 133–5; need for love, 80–1; reasons why few for adoption, 7–8; response to change, 134

background information: adopters' need for, 110; need for reticence with neighbours, 129; requests for more, 178

bedwetting, 140, 143

*Be My Parent* books, 5, 6, 99

birth parents: adopters' feelings about, 56–7, 123, 177, 179; agreement to adoption, 11, 87–9; child's feelings about, 172, 177–9; giving information about, 177–9; meeting with adopters, 122–3; used as a threat by child, 160–1; varied circumstances of, 58–64

black children: books for, 104, 164; grooming, 104, 164; growing up in white families, 163–4; need for black families, 8, 10; need for positive image, 45, 163

British Agencies for Adoption and Fostering, 94, 176, 178

carelessness, 83

caretakers, problems in parting with child, 127–8

changes, seen as criticism, 151

child abuse, 63–4

Children Act (1975): access to birth records, 180; adoption allowances, 10; freeing for adoption, 11, 89; prohibition of placement by individuals, 93; the welfare principle, 88

children's homes, 83, 125